QUAKERS OBSERVED IN PROSE AND VERSE

D1630501

The cover design is courtesy of The Library of the Religious Society of Friends, London (85/N 19)
Silhouette of Elizabeth Wright, born Ingle (1820-1880).

for

GILLIE AND ANDREW

ANTHONY AND ROSEMARY

Quakers Observed

in

Prose and Verse

An Anthology
1656 – 1986

Compiled and Edited by

Mollie Grubb

William Sessions Limited
York, England

ISBN 1 85072 122 X

F78

Printed in 10 on 11 point Bembo Typeface
by William Sessions Limited
The Ebor Press
York, England

Contents

		Page
Editor's Note and Acknowledgements		vi
Introduction		vii
Chapter I The Seventeenth Century		1
Chapter II The Eighteenth Century		13
Chapter III The Nineteenth Century		58
Chapter IV The Twentieth Century		98
Reference and Notes		117
List of Contributors		119
Index		120

Illustrations

Title page of Anti-Quaker Tract 54
[COURTESY OF WOODBROOKE COLLEGE LIBRARY, BIRMINGHAM]

Joshua Kaye (1773?-1851) of Leeds 55
[COURTESY OF FRIENDS HOUSE LIBRARY]

Engraving by Rowlandson & Pugin (1809) 56
[COURTESY OF FRIENDS HOUSE LIBRARY]

John Porter Rodwell, Quaker Missionary, c.1910 57
[COURTESY OF JOANNA KIRKBY]

Editor's Note and Acknowledgements

THE ANTHOLOGY is not exhaustive and for various reasons it has not been possible to use all the material suggested to me. With a few exceptions the extracts are taken from contemporary sources and are arranged chronologically by date of publication, so that changes in attitudes towards Quakers may be more easily followed through the centuries.

I am most grateful to all those who have contributed with references and suggestions; a list of contributors may be found at the end of the book and if anyone has inadvertently been omitted I sincerely apologise. I should like to thank David Blamires for the use of the title and to acknowledge the courteous assistance I have received from the staff of the Language and Literature Department of Birmingham Central Library, Woodbrooke College Library and Friends House Library. My warm thanks also go to Helen Davidson for the original idea, to Joy Povolny and Joan Butcher, to my typist Penny Robinson and especially to Joanna Kirkby for all the work we did together, her constructive criticism and finally help with proof reading.

Every effort has been made to trace the authors or publishers of the extracts used, but in some instances this has not been successful. The author is most grateful to all who are quoted in the following pages whose names together with book titles and publishers are in all cases mentioned in appreciative acknowledgement.

May 1993   Mollie Grubb

Introduction

THE CASUAL READER of this Anthology may be amused, interested and perhaps shocked, while a more serious, consecutive reading of the passages chosen will reveal a steady change and development in the attitudes of the 'world's people' towards Quakers. The Introduction, therefore, is intended only briefly to provide a setting for these passages and to make the views expressed intelligible in the general context of a particular period.

The movement George Fox founded in the turbulent years of the latter half of the 17th century has been described as 'one of the most remarkable and dynamic movements in English religious history'.[1] In total opposition to the established beliefs and practices of the time, Fox gave to those who heeded him the hope of personal unity with their Creator independent of priest or ritual. A vital part of the Quaker message was that in discarding the centuries-old structure of the church so as to return to the simplicity of the original gospel teaching Quakerism not only proclaimed the 'Truth' but claimed the sole right to its possession; such a claim makes intelligible the opposition aroused within the Anglican church and by Presbyterian divines like Richard Baxter and caused a violent tract war. Apart from some extracts from Baxter's ONE SHEET AGAINST THE QUAKERS which is of theological interest, these tracts have not been included in the Anthology; they are often abusive and denunciatory in their language, the points they raise lengthy and obscure.

The claims made for Quakerism led to the accusations of pride which appear in the early entries. What was meant was spiritual pride, the belief that Quakers possessed a unique relationship with God independent of priest and ritual and which seemed to the outsider to claim spiritual superiority. The accusations of enthusiasm and fanaticism made against Quakers were a result of their uneasy situation within the calm rationalism of the Enlightenment. When John Evelyn calls them 'phanatic' he is describing the extravagance of their religious claims. An additional reason for the hostility encountered by early Quakers lay in what amounted to civil disobedience. Their refusal to pay tithes or to take oaths brought them into conflict with both the priesthood and the law of the land. It was not only by the authorities that they were seen as a threat. In the extract from Anthony a Wood, for example, the congregation rushed panic-stricken from the church on the rumour that the Quakers were coming, a reflection both of the forcefulness with which their beliefs were sometimes expounded and the disorder which must often have ensued when Quakers used their right under the Directory of Public Worship of 1645 to criticise the minister after, and sometimes during his sermon.

In spite of opposition the movement gathered strength and the great public gatherings held by George Fox, Edward Burrough, Francis Howgill and others of the early Friends, which became known as 'threshing meetings', attracted vast crowds, sometimes numbering several thousand people. It has been estimated that at the time of the restoration of Charles II in 1660 Quaker men, women and children numbered some 30 or 40 thousand out of a total population of about five million.[2] A calculation on a similar basis made today would give a total membership of about 400 thousand instead of the 18 thousand or so the Society actually numbers, a comparison which will give some idea of the wide appeal of Quakerism in the 17th century. Religion at that time dominated the minds of the people to an extent not seen in England before or since, the huge public meetings to be likened perhaps to crowds gathering to watch a modern sporting fixture.

Persecution under the Clarendon Code caused suffering and distress, to which were added the accusations of lechery and hypocrisy described by David Blamires and Derek Forbes. Quakers were the target of persecution by both church and state, unprotected from popular abuse. The accusation of lechery was almost certainly a consequence of the Quakers' total rejection of the marriage ceremony celebrated by a priest; no matter how solemnly Quakers regarded the binding tie witnessed to in the meeting for worship, in the eyes of the world they were merely sinful. There was, too, a feeling that the moral standards Quakers set themselves were impossible of attainment by ordinary men and women, they must be hypocrites and there was undoubtedly rejoicing if a Quaker was suspected of having feet of clay. But Restoration England was licentious and depraved by any standards and due weight should be given to the feelings of resentment aroused by men and women who set themselves patterns of belief and conduct different from the society of which they formed part. The accusation of hypocrisy has lingered on through the centuries. It is hinted at in the otherwise sympathetic treatment of Quakers in SYLVIA'S LOVERS, in which Mrs Gaskell shows the Quaker brothers as not above dealing in smuggled goods (a problem which worried successive sessions of London Yearly Meeting in the late18th century); it is not dead even today and is reflected in Bertrand Russell's earliest view of Quakers, which unfortunately it has not been possible to include. Against this accusation should be set, in the 17th century, the calm assessment of Celia Fiennes as she journeyed round the country and Lady Anne Conway, who preferred quiet Quakers as her servants. Matthew Green in his early 18th-century verses in praise of Robert Barclay's APOLOGY finds Quaker theology attractive but Quaker ways too difficult in practice; he would like to follow them, but: 'Like you I think, but cannot live'. The radical pamphleteer Daniel Defoe, writing during the 1720's, sometimes portrays Quakers as good and kindly people; he does not comment on their religious principles but does try to show Quaker goodness in contrast with the depravity of the age in which he lived. As the 18th century progressed attitudes towards Quakers tended to become more approving, until near its close a Quaker was portrayed on the stage as a serious and thoroughly worthy hero, something which would have been impossible in earlier drama.

There were several reasons why this should have taken place. When persecution of Quakers virtually ceased with the Toleration Act of 1689 they themselves became altogether more restrained in their behaviour. A set of beliefs one has inherited, as did these second and third generation Quakers, is rarely so compelling as the truth hewn out in the arena of conflict and disputation. Gone was the fierce proselytising of the early days and the Society settled down to consolidate its position within the structure of church government devised by George Fox. Ministers continued to travel round the country preaching the Quaker message, but the evangelical fervour of the early years had greatly quietened down. It is sometimes said that Quakers in the 18th century retired behind a 'hedge' of peculiarities which they erected against the world; they did regard themselves as 'not of this world' and continued to do so through the 19th century but it is equally true to say that they found themselves increasingly isolated in the world of the Enlightenment. They were still regarded as 'enthusiasts' by David Hume and their form of worship, the direct communion with God in the silence of the meeting, the emphasis they placed on the mystical idea of unity with God,[3] the illumination of the Inner Light, were inimical to the calm rationalism of the 18th century, while to the ordinary man or woman the standards of morality and behaviour they set themselves were still objects of ridicule.

Two factors at least may have helped to bring about their greater social acceptability during the century. The first is related to the Quaker principle of plain dress. This was originally the every-day dress of the 17th century, stripped of its ornament, but because Quakers were not meant to be influenced by changing fashions it became through the years a kind of uniform, setting the Quaker apart from his or her fellows. But the Quaker woman, in her simple, plain dress, kerchief and bonnet presented a marked and tantalising contrast to the fashionable beauty, so as to inspire the sentimental response of such verses as 'The Fair Quakers' and in 1806 Lord Byron's lines 'To a Beautiful Quaker'. However Quaker men were regarded, Quaker women were all that was beautiful, good and desirable. Secondly, the plain and simple truth on which Quakers insisted meant that business could be done with them with a degree of security frequently lacking during that period. The Quaker's 'Yea' was yea, his 'Nay' was nay, he did not bargain or cheat and a child could be entrusted to use his shop. To do business with Quakers became sought after, they began to be respected and to accumulate wealth and the foundation of several Quaker fortunes, for example that of the banking Lloyds, was laid in the 18th century. This is illustrated very clearly in Mrs Gaskell's treatment of the Quaker brothers in SYLVIA'S LOVERS.

There had been a movement towards social reform in the work of the philanthropist John Bellers (1654-1725) early in the 18th century, but it was not until the evangelical movement began to make its impact on the Society towards the end of the century that Friends started to break away from their long period of isolation and move out into the world. Their peculiarities of worship, speech and dress still set Quakers apart, but gaps were beginning to appear in the 'hedge'. Perhaps the first notable contribution to the acceptance of Quakers as concerned not merely for the welfare of their own sect but for the welfare of mankind in general lies in the work of Elizabeth Fry among the women prisoners in Newgate gaol and her subsequent involvement in prison reform; here was a woman stepping outside the narrow confines of a particular religious group to devote her life to her fellows of any religious persuasion or none and the admiration she aroused may be judged from the reaction of the usually sceptical Sydney Smith. To the late 18th and early 19th centuries also belongs Quaker involvement in the anti-slavery campaign, acknowledged by Sir Thomas Fowell Buxton. It is noteworthy that in 1783 London Yearly Meeting approved a petition to parliament declaring the trade illegal[4] and Friends and the Society's network of monthly meetings were behind Wilberforce and the Anti-Slavery Committee.

The man and the woman in the street still poked fun at Quakers and Quaker ways in verses like THE QUAKER'S MEETING by Samuel Lover and in Mrs Craik's JOHN HALIFAX GENTLEMAN we are given a portrait of a Quaker who is totally stern, uncompromising and lacking in humanity. But people of greater perception, like Thomas Carlyle, valued Quaker principles and practices. As the 19th century advanced opinion of Quakers continued to be divided, as witnessed by William Cobbett's savage attack on Quaker business transactions, but such outright condemnation became the exception rather than the rule. By the mid-century the 'hedge' had to a large extent disappeared and Friends found themselves more at ease in the climate of the age. They became involved in the adult-school movement and their activity in movements for social reform is attested by the great 19th-century reformers Josephine Butler and Octavia Hill.[5] Irish famine relief in 1846 was the forerunner of the relief work which came to maturity in the 20th century. In the light of Friends' increasing social involvement it was curious that George Borrow in 1851 should consider Quakers 'a decaying sect' who did 'good work in their day', while at the close of the century Michael Fairless also considered that 'in a few short years the word Quaker will sound as strange in our ears as the older appellation Shaker does now'. The gentle melancholy of Michael Fairless's evocation of Quaker quietness and peace seems to sound the death knell of the Society and both she and George Borrow were clearly aware of the tensions within 19th-century Quakerism, but the Society survived to enter upon a new century in which its historic peace testimony became a dominant theme.

The paucity of material for the 20th century does not refect a falling away of interest in Quakers. This is still very much alive and any tendency towards ridicule has disappeared; where Quakers are observed it is with seriousness. Rose Macaulay obliquely, and Arnold Toynbee explicitly have seen Quakers as 'a yeast which has not yet leavened the lump'. But Rose Macaulay's portrait of Barry, burdened with committee work, suggested early in the century that the Society was losing its way in what the Quietists called 'creaturely activity'; Iris Murdoch portrays Quakers as fallen away from their beliefs, as lapsed Quakers who, even in their willingness to live on the surface of life without seeking its deeper meaning, sometimes glimpse the Light by which they once lived; the accusation of shallowness may also be seen in her description of Ennistone Friends and their refusal to explore the concept of the Inner Light. Christopher Isherwood, in THE WORLD IN THE EVENING, portrays a character who, however much he tries to reject Quakerism, cannot entirely free himself from its residual influence, while Nan, in Rose Macaulay's DANGEROUS AGES, realises that the Christian life might be 'a fine and adventurous thing to live'.

But because the 20th century has seen two horrific world wars and because violence has become in many parts of the world almost a way of life, the Society's historic peace testimony has become a dominant issue among Friends and one whose implications have thrust Quakers into the forefront of public opinion. Edward Grubb, the treasurer of the No Conscription Fellowship, won the admiration of Bertrand Russell, while her friendship with the Quaker Corder Catchpool and his family was of value to Vera Brittain during the second world war. In 1957 Harry Emerson Fosdick described Quaker pacifism as 'positive, constructive and socially-minded', Arnold Toynbee had whole-hearted approval for George Cadbury's stand in the first world war and in 1986 Fenner Brockway was associated with the visit of the Northern Friends Peace Board to what was then the Soviet Union. But in THE GAME A. S. Byatt draws attention to the difficulty of maintaining a strict adherence to the peace testimony in the face of the determined use of force.

The theme of this anthology, therefore, has been one of changing attitudes, of the slow emergence of Quakers into the mainstream of society and society's slow acceptance of them. Today, Quakers seem generally to be regarded as peacemakers and I think it is legitimate to ask at this point whether the peace testimony, difficult to hold and vitally important though it is, will suffice to carry the Society forward in a deeply troubled world. This testimony has its roots in a religious movement of great spiritual depth. Do we today place sufficient emphasis on our spiritual heritage? Are we content with the way we are observed?

CHAPTER I

The Seventeenth Century

JOHN EVELYN (1620-1706) was a much respected and admired friend of Samuel Pepys, although his DIARY is by no means so racy and entertaining. He also knew Thomas Ellwood, a young gentleman of family working as a clerk for Pepys in the Navy Office and a good Latinist. When John Milton began to lose his sight, he asked John Evelyn to find him an amanuensis – who needed to be a good Latinist. Evelyn mentioned the matter to Pepys and eventually Ellwood became Milton's scribe. Later, of course, as a Quaker he wrote THE LIFE OF GEORGE FOX. The following is the only reference to Quakers in John Evelyn's DIARY:

1656. July 10th, Ipswich. I had the curiosity to visit some Quakers here in prison: a new phanatic sect, of dangerous principles, who shew no respect to any man, magistrate or other, and seem a melancholy proud★ sort of people, and exceedingly ignorant. One of these was said to have fasted 20 daies, but another endeavouring to do the same, perished on 10th, when he would have eaten but could not.

The following extract is from THE LIFE AND TIMES OF ANTHONY À WOOD (1624-1695), antiquarian and historian:

[1659] July 31, Sunday, a terrible wind hapned in the afternoon, while all people were at divine service. Two or three stones, and some rough-cast stuff were blown off the tower of S. Martin alias Carfax and falling on the leads of the church, a great alarm and out-cry was among the people in the church. Some cried 'murder!' – and at that time a trumpet or trumpets sounding neare the Cross-inne dore, to call the soldiers together, because of the present plott,† they in the church cried out that the day of judgment was at hand. Some said the anabaptists

---

★The accusation of pride may be found in much anti-Quaker writing of this early period.
†The 'present plott' was probably one of the numerous plots to bring about the restoration of Charles II, of which, according to the Diary of Samuel Pepys, the country was full.

and quakers were come to cut their throats while the preacher, Mr George Philips, perceiving their errour, was ready to burst into laughter in the pulpit, to see such a confusion, and several of the people that were in the galleries hanging at the bottom of them and falling on the heads of people crowding on the floor to get out of dores [*sic*].

John Bunyan *(1628-1688), the son of a tinsmith, was born at Elstow near Bedford and was put to his father's respectable trade at an early age. When he was about 17 he was drafted into the Parliamentary army, an experience probably reflected in his THE HOLY WAR. He later became a Baptist minister and was a charismatic preacher, becoming known playfully round his native Bedford as 'Bishop Bunyan'. He was imprisoned in November 1660 for preaching without a licence and remained there for 12 years, until Charles II's Declaration of Indulgence. During the first half of this period he wrote nine of his books, including GRACE ABOUNDING FOR THE CHIEF OF SINNERS (1666) from which the first extract from his work is taken. THE PILGRIM'S PROGRESS was completed in two volumes in 1678, the first part having been written during another short period of imprisonment:*

GRACE ABOUNDING FOR THE CHIEF OF SINNERS

Also, besides teaching of God in His Word, the Lord made use of two things to confirm me in these things; the one was the error of the Quakers, and the other was the guilt of sin; for as the Quakers did oppose His truth, so God did the more confirm me in it, by leading me into the scriptures that did wonderfully maintain it. (p 123)

The errors that this people [the Quakers] then maintained were: 1. That the Holy Scriptures were not the Word of God. 2. That every man in the world had the spirit of Christ, grace, faith, etc. 3. That Christ Jesus, as crucified, and dying 1,600 years ago, did not satisfy divine justice for the sins of the people. 4. That Christ's flesh and blood was within the saints. 5. That the bodies of the good and bad that are buried in the churchyard should not rise again. 6. That the resurrection is past with good men already. 7. That the man Jesus, that was crucified between two thieves on Mount Calvary, in the land of Canaan, by Jerusalem, was not ascended above the starry heavens. 8. That He should not, even the same Jesus that died by the hands of the Jews, come again at the last day, and as man judge all the nations, etc. (p 142)

Many more vile and abominable things were in those days fomented by them, by which I was driven to a more narrow search of the Scriptures . . . (p 125)

The Pilgrims *meet the* Flatterer. *William York Tindale in* JOHN BUNYAN, MECHANICK PREACHER, *1934, p.64, suggests that in his portrayal of the Flatterer Bunyan intends an attack upon Quakers. The charge of hypocrisy was commonly levelled against them well into the 18th century:*

They went then till they came to a place where they saw a Way put itself into their Way, and seemed withal to lie as straight as the Way which they should go; and here they knew not which of the two to take, for both seemed straight before them; therefore they stood still to consider. And as they were thinking about the Way, behold a man of black flesh, but covered with a very light robe, came to them, and asked them why they stood there? They answered they were going to the Celestial City, but knew not which of these Ways to take. 'Follow me,' said the man, 'it is thither that I am going.' So they followed him in the Way that but now came into a road, which by degrees turned, and turned them so from the City that they decided to go to, that in a little time their faces were turned away from it: – yet they followed him. But by and by, before they were aware, he led them both within the compass of a net, in which they were both so entangled that they knew not what to do; and with that the white robe fell off the black mans back: then they saw where they were. Wherefore there they lay crying for some time, for they could not get themselves out. . . .

Thus they lay bewailing themselves in the net. At last they espied a Shining One coming towards them with a whip of small cord in his hand. When he was come to the place where they were, he asked them whence they came, and what they did there? They told him they were poor pilgrims going to ZION, but were led out of the way by a black man clothed in white, who bid us, said they, follow him, for he was going thither too. Then said he with the whip, It is the Flatterer, 'a false apostle that hath transformed himself into an angel of light'. So he rent the net, and let the men out. (pp 182-4)

THE DIARY OF SAMUEL PEPYS (1633-1703)

31 October 1665: [*The Great Plague of 1665*] In the City died this week 7,496 and of them 6,102 of the plague. But it is feared that the true number of the dead this week is near 10,000, partly from the poor that cannot be taken notice of through the greatness of their number and partly from the Quakers and others that will not have any bell ring for them.

29 July 1667: To Westminster Hall, where the Hall full of people to see the issue of the day, the King being come to speak to the House today. One thing extraordinary was, this day a man, a Quaker, came almost naked through the

Hall, and with a chafing-dish of fire and brimstone burning upon his head, did pass through the Hall, crying 'Repent! repent!'

21 December 1667: At the office [*the Navy Office*] all the morning, and at noon home to dinner with my Clerks and Creed [*Pepys' friend and colleague*], who among other things all alone after dinner, talking of the times, he tells me that the Nonconformists are mighty high, and their meetings frequent and connived at; and they do expect to have their day now soon, for my Lord of Buckingham is a declared friend to them, and even to the Quakers, who had very good words the other day from the King himself.

29 December 1667: At the night comes Mrs Turner to see us; and there among other talk she tells me that Mr William Pen [*sic*] who is lately come over from Ireland, is a Quaker again, or some such very melancholy thing; that he cares for no company, nor comes in to any. . . .

12 October 1668: So to supper and after supper to read a ridiculous nonsensical book set out by William Pen,★ for the Quakers, but so full of nothing but nonsense that I was ashamed to read in it.

12 February 1669: . . . and so home and there Pelling hath got me W. Pen's book against the Trinity.† I got my wife to read it to me [*Pepys was going blind*], and I find it so well writ as, I think, it is too good for him ever to have writ it, and it is a serious sort of book, and not fit for everybody to read.

Pepys was clearly curious about Quakers and towards the end of his DIARY *reveals a perhaps reluctant admiration for William Penn, whose father Admiral Sir William Penn he heartily disliked. It is unfortunate that his blindness forced him to abandon his* DIARY *in 1669, or he might have left us with additional vivid glimpses of his Quaker contemporaries.*

ADVENTURES BY SEA – Edward Coxere (1633-1694)

This JOURNAL, *which tells the life story of the 17th-century seaman* EDWARD COXERE, *can according to E. H. W. Meyerstein be placed somewhere between April 1685 and the writer's death in October 1694. He was converted to Quakerism by Edward Burrough and Samuel Fisher and the following extract describes his encounter with them and with Luke Howard (1621-1699), the father of Dover meeting:*

★This book was TRUTH EXALTED . . . by W. Penn.
†This book was A SANDY FOUNDATION SHAKEN. Its publication without licence caused William Penn to be committed to the Tower.

I being now at home with my family, to spend some time till another freight presented, two men called Quakers came to our town at Dover, Samuel Fisher and Edw. Burows. William Rusell, a priest, and they were to have a dispute in Jame's Church, so called. I, understanding of it, met with William White, that were second mate of the ship I went chief mate of. I told him the priest and the Quakers were to have a dispute; I got him along with me to hear them. Edward Burows undertook the dispute with the priest, telling him that though he was not brought up at the University, yet he did not question but the Lord would make him able to answer him in the vindication of God's truth, or words to this purpose. My mind being set to hear both parties, gave as good attention as I could, insomuch that the Lord at that time visited my soul and reached my very inward parts, so that my understanding was something opened, that my affec-tions drew to the principle the Quaker held forth to be more sound than the priest's. Now there were many people hearers; I took notice of them, and such as I knew to be the rudest sort of people despised the Quakers and held with the priest. This confirmed me the more; the Lord let me see it to my farther convince-ment. This was not all, but the Lord in his mercy followed me that very day, and brought not peace but trouble; for the first remarkable opening I had before I slept from the Lord was concerning fighting and killing of enemies. The ques-tioning the lawfulness or unlawfulness of it lay on me as a very great burden, because it struck at my very life. . . .

I got to Luke Howard's house in the evening, where these two men were to seek for ease, and told them I was a seaman and upon going to sea, we having wars, and should we meet with an enemy whether or no I might lawfully fight. They, being very mild, used but few words, I being a stranger to them, but wished me to be faithful to what the Lord did make known to me, and words to that purpose, so did not encourage me to fight, but left me to the working of the power of the Lord in my own heart, which was more prevalent than words in the condition I then was in; so that I did not lay down fighting on other men's words, but the Lord taught me to love my enemies in his own time. This work was not done at once, for the Enemy of my soul, under whom I had been a soldier so long, striving to kill men who I never saw nor had any prejudice against, as the manner of the wars is, and then take their goods as my own, for so I have done and so I have been served, now the Lord giving me a little glimmering of the unlawfulness of it, I saw I had a very heavy cross to take up, and it was indeed; it was so heavy that I could not soon take it up; I was yet too weak.[1]

The following extract relates an experience Edward Coxere had after he became a Quaker and is included as an illustration of what must have been a popular view of the Society. As in the extract from Anthony à Wood, it is an example of the fear in which Quakers were held by common people:

There was then [1661] but few Friends masters of ships. I understanding that Edmond Tiddeman was bound to sea, I wrote to him to know if he would be willing to accept of me to go as his mate. He answered me 'Very willing'. He then did not come among Friends. His wife's mother, which was old William

Stratford's wife, soon heard of it, for it was noised abroad as a dangerous thing to carry a Quaker to sea, fearing he should also become one too. They used their endeavours to prevent it, but did not take effect. The old woman, being disturbed, sent for me to her house, where I found the old woman and the old man together, where the old woman would a persuaded me not to go to sea with her son, telling me that she had said her prayers often in the night, desiring to be satisfied, but could not unless I would promise her not to go to sea with her son, lest he should become a Quaker, and then what merchants would employ him?[2]

THE JOURNEYS OF CELIA FIENNES

Celia Fiennes *(1662-1741) was the granddaughter of the first Viscount Saye and Sele. She was advised to travel for her health and in the late 17th and early 18th centuries made a number of long journeys around England. Coming from a nonconformist background she was on the whole tolerant of Quakers, although she notes a little acidly of a Quaker meeting at Scarborough that* 'their prayers were all made in the first person single':

pp 73-74, 1697: Thence we went to Mansfield 12 mile and pass'd some part of the fine Forrest of Sherwood. Mansfield is a little Market town built with stone, there is a little river, they make and dry Tammy's here; there is one pretty stone built house just by the waterside of 40 stepps ascent to it; at the end of the town is an hospital built by a quaker for ancient people, its a good neat building they were to have 8 pound a year a piece and the roomes and gardens, but its chiefly for their friends . . .

p 89, 1697: From thence [Hull] to Beverly againe 6 mile which is all a flatt, thence to Brance Burton [*Brandesburton*] 8 mile and likewise on a Levell which they call Lough; here we could get no accommodation at a Publick house, it being a a poore thatch'd place and only 2 or 3 sorry Ale-houses, no lodgings but at the Hall House as it was called, where liv'd a Quaker which were sufficient people, the rooms were good old rooms being the Lord of the Mannours house; these were but tennants but did entertain us kindly, made two good beds for us also for our servants, and good bread and cheese and bacon and eggs . . .

pp 92-93, 1697: The town [Scarborough] has abundance of Quakers in it, most of their best lodgings were in Quaker hands, they entertain all people soe in Private houses in the town, by way of ordinary,* so much a Meale, and their Ale every one finds themselves, there are a few Inns for horses only. I was at a Quaker Meeting in the town where 4 men and 2 women spoke, one after another had

*In 17th-century England, the serving of a meal at a public house.

done, but it seem'd such a confusion and so incoherent that it very much moved my companion to pitty to see their delusion and ignorance, and no less excited my thankfullness for the Grace of God that upheld others from such Errors; I observ'd their prayers were all made in the first person single, tho' before the body of people, it seems they allow not of ones being the mouth of the rest in prayer to God tho' it be in the public meetings . . .

p 143, 1698: [*At Colchester*] . . . mostly old buildings except a few builded by some Quakers that are brick and of London mode . . . the town did extend itself to the sea but now its ruines sets it 3 miles off; the low grounds all about the town are used for whitening their Bayes for which this town is remarkable, and also for exceeding good oysters, but its a deare place and to gratifye my curiosity to eat them in the place I paid dear; its a town full of Dessenters 2 meetings very full besides Anabaptists and Quakers . . .

p 253, 1698: *She notes that at Plymouth there were* '4 Large Meetings for the Dessenters in the town, takeing in the Quakers and Anabaptists'.

> [Quakers and Anabaptists were linked together by Celia Fiennes and separated from other Dissenters, presumably because Anabaptists admitted only adult baptism as against the wider practice of infant baptism; Quakers of course rejected the need for baptism altogether. This practice of linking the two sects together may have been common at this early period.]

QUAKERS OBSERVED IN PROSE AND VERSE – David Blamires
Included in A QUAKER MISCELLANY FOR EDWARD MILLIGAN, 1985

This contribution to the Miscellany examines aspects of the conduct and moral values attributed to Quakers in the latter half of the 17th century . Dryden's satirical allegory, THE HIND AND THE PANTHER (1687), *commenting on the religious and political issues of the time, gives Puritans, Roman Catholics and the Church of England full and lengthy treatment, while Quakers are dismissed in the following couplet:*

> Among the timorous kind the Quaking Hare
> Profess'd neutrality but would not swear (1. 37-38).

David Blamires *points out that the hare is not merely a timorous and shrinking creature, but is also associated with witchcraft and lechery and the licentious nature of some of the songs and jokes to which he refers shows that in the popular view Quakers were indeed seen as lechers in the early years of the Society.*

But it has to be remembered that post-Restoration England is notorious for its licentiousness and excess. The mere fact that Quakers set themselves higher standards than the norm would be sufficient to make them the target of slander and ridicule, as will be clear from their portrayal upon the stage in the drama of the following century.

7

THE WEAKER VESSEL *by Antonia Fraser, published in 1984, explores the position of women in the 17th century.*

Antonia Fraser *(1932-   ) begins her 'author's note' to this book by referring to a male friend who questioned whether in fact there were any notable women in 17th-century England. It was clearly a relief and a pleasure to her to find George Fox and the Quakers asserting that (a) females had souls, (b) females should and could preach and (c) females had a great work to do, working with men in 'God's Vineyard', in organisation, caring for the poor and, in the letters from prison of the Quaker Elizabeth Hooton, anticipating by 150 years the demands of the 19th-century prison reformer Elizabeth Fry. It is noteworthy that in 1656 George Fox published his tract THE WOMAN LEARNING IN SILENCE, which, while it enjoined women to be submissive to their husbands, also emphasised their spiritual equality –* 'for in that Male where Christ doth reign, rule and speak, he will own Christ in the Female'. *Antonia Fraser notes that this is the first such defence of women since the Reformation.*[3]

Chapter 18 of her book recounts with approval and in great detail the work of prominent women Quakers like Elizabeth Hooton, Mary Fisher, Margaret Fell (who became known as the 'nursing mother' of Quakerism) and the Fell daughters, lives of great interest in the history of the long struggle of women for independence from male domination, and describes how their countrymen and women reacted to them. We are told, for example, that Anne, Viscountess Conway, who herself became a Quaker before her death:

Desired to have [Quaker] servants about her because this 'suffering people', so 'still and very serious in their behaviour' would make ideal sympathetic attendants for an invalid.[4]

Lord Conway on the other hand, in Ireland where he had to cope with the Quakers' sudden demonstrations according to the dictates of the 'inner Light', found them 'senseless, wilful, ridiculous'.

There is little doubt that some Quaker women, in the enjoyment of their new found freedom to make their voices heard, went too far and the violence of their behaviour and vociferous preaching did nothing to allay 'hostility to a religion which relied on the worrying instrument of extempore prayer – uncontrollable from the outside.'[5] *John Punshon, however, considers such strictures undeserved –* 'Where they did preach in churches, they either did so by invitation or because they claimed the right to do so under the 'Directory', after the minister had finished his sermon',[6] *but it seems possible that overzealous Quakers, both men and women, did not always wait to be given leave.*

The hostility aroused by a new and strange form of religious worship led not infrequently to charges of witchcraft, as has been observed in the material examined by David Blamires (see page 7), and Antonia Fraser cites the Royalist pamphleteer John Nalsen in THE COUNTERMINE:

That such impromptu manifestations were in fact inspired by the devil. He gave an instance of a woman who had become generally admired for being 'so eminent in this Gift of Prayer', subsequently she went to New England where she was discovered to be 'a most Abominable Witch'. At her trial she confessed that she had given up her soul to the devil in return for the gift of extemporary prayer. Concluded Nalsen with satisfaction: 'Either now we believe that the Extempore Way is not an infallible sign of the Spirit of God: or that the Devil has the Power of disposing of the Gifts of the Spirit'.[7]

Yet Quaker women continued brave and steadfast, even although being called upon to endure imprisonment in the horror of 17th-century gaols and, in the case of Mary Dyer, death by hanging on Boston Common in New England in 1659.

Those in authority were not always hostile to the Quakers. When Mary Fisher felt called by the Holy Spirit to visit the Sultan of Turkey in 1657 she was listened to with respect, the truth of some part at least of her message was acknowledged and she was sent graciously on her way. Elizabeth Hooton was received with courtesy by Charles II and Antonia Fraser gives an account of a scene witnessed by Samuel Pepys, when a pretty young Quaker wife, cheated out of her fortune by a dissolute and absconding husband, was kindly received by the king. (But one wonders whether it was Charles' sympathy for Quakers or his weakness for a pretty face which promoted his concern.)

<hr>

ONE SHEET AGAINST THE QUAKERS – *Richard Baxter (1615-1791)*

For those concerned with the theological arguments against Quakerism some extracts from this book, written in 1657, may be of interest. Richard Baxter was a nonconformist divine and parliamentarian, but he had no employment under the Protectorate and was probably among those who plotted for the return of Charles II. On Charles' accession to the throne he was offered the bishopric of Hereford. He wrote a number of books on religious subjects, including the well-known RELIQUAE BAXTERIANÆ. *Although he was of course sympathetic towards other nonconformists it appears that he did not understand the mysticism implicit in the concept of the inner Light. In his book he lists 24 reasons why no reasonable man should be a Quaker. A great many of them are protests against Quaker attacks on 'hireling priests' and the payment of tithes, so the following is only a small selection of the most interesting:*

Reason 1.   The Quakers (with the Seekers) deny and revile the Church and ministers of Christ, and yet cannot tell us of any church or ministry which is indeed the right, and to be preferred before those that they despise. If the Quakers are of no church themselves, they are no Christians, and they are infidels, atheists or heathen. If they be of the church, let them tell us which is the church they are of. They renounce the church that we are of; and that is the only church on earth, containing all true believers in Christ. They have not told us of any sect but their own, which they take to be the true church; and he that takes the Quakers to be the only catholic church, must deny the church and Christ himself,

9

if he understand what he saith. For the Quakers are but of a few years standing; they rose from among Papists, Seekers, Ranters and Anabaptists. . . .

Reason 2. No wise man can be Quaker, because their Religion is an uncertain thing; And so is not the Religion that must save us. The things that they agree in, besides the furious opposition of others, are but a few broken scraps of Doctrine, which they never yet set together, as making the substance of their faith. I never met with any man that heard of any sum or body of their Divinity, Faith or Religion, which they have published . . . Nor did I ever hear that one of their Speakers did ever recite the substance of their belief. If they know not yet the contents of their own Religion, they are too [*sic*] blame to be zealous for it, and thrust that upon others, which they know not themselves: and well may we stay till they know it better, before we become their followers for we know not what. The Christian faith is known long ago, even this 1600 years and more. If they say that they wait till the spirit revealeth it, I answer, the spirit hath revealed and sealed the Christian faith long ago: though it must transcribe it out of the Scripture into the heart of every believer. The Spirit is not given now to make us a new religion, or new Gospels, *Gal. 1:8,9,* but to cause us to believe and receive the old one . . . Well, but will any but a mad man let go of his Christian Faith before he know where to have a better? of for he knows not what? Shall we turn Quakers meerly [*sic*] because they bark and howl at our Religion, Ministry and Church, before they tell where to find a better . . .

Reason 8. The Quakers way is too cruel and uncharitable to be the way of God. They damn the most humble, holy, and faithful servants of God, to whom God hath promised salvation. All the Ministers and Churches of Christ that adhere to the Ministry, they pronounce them, children of the Devil: and as soon as they do but hear a man speak for the Ministry, though they know nothing of his life, they can presently [*at the moment*] tell that he is a Hypocrite and a child of the Devil; so quick and sagacious they are in damning men, as if they were as forward to it as Christ to save, add [*sic*] pleased as much in cursing good men as in blessing. Yea they must venture into the Throne of God, and ordinarily take on them to know men's hearts, to judge them hypocrites. Those that dwell with God, have laid longer at his feet in prayer and tears, then [*sic*] any of them, and will walk in uprightness in the midst of a malicious world, and spend themselves in the Work of God; even these must be damned at a word by a boy or wench that's but a Quaker, as confidently as if God have bid them speak it.

Reasons 10. And in this and many other Doctrines, they do openly comply with the Papists, that we may plainly see that the Jesuits and Fryers are their Leaders . . . the Papists make the Scriptures a dead letter, no sufficient Rule or Faith, or Judge of Controversies; and so do they. The Papists cry down the Church and Ministry, and so do they. The Jesuits cry up free-will and sufficient grace to all, and a common sufficient Light, and so do they . . .

Reason 11.   Their doctrines are self-contradictory, and therefore they cannot be of God. They say that all men have a sufficient light within them, and yet they go up and down preaching, with great zeal and insolence. And what do they preach? Is it light or darkness? If darkness, who would have such preachers? If light, what needless labour is this, when all men have sufficient light already? And will they revile the ministers as blind guides, and tell their people they are all in darkness, and the way to damnation? And yet all have sufficient light within them? If all, why not the ministers and their people? Are they not men?

Reason 23.   Moreover, the way by which they prevail, is not by producing any evidence: For they renounce that, and offer you all on the Authority of the Spirit within them: and therefore they must prove the Authority, and their Revelations and Divine Mission by Miracles, or such supernatural means, before any reasonable man can believe them. Unless you will believe every man that hath faith, he is sent of God. I have asked them to shew their Commission from God, or prove that he sent them, and not one of them would ever do it, but tell me I was blind, and he had the witness in himself; But why must I believe him that saith this more than other men? Can I see the witness in him? It must be a witness to me if he will have credit. But Ministers of Christ do not call you to receive their doctrine upon the Authority of themselves or their own Mission, but of the Apostles and their Mission, from whom they had it and who sealed it with Miracles long go: And therefore whether we were Ministers or no, you have reason to believe us, when we prove our Doctrine to be from God, as delivered by the Apostles and Scripture, and Sealed by the Spirit: But Quakers that give us their Doctrine on a new Authority within them (and so Behmenists, Paracelsians and all Enthusiasts) and Papists that give it us on their own Authority as above or before Scripture Authority, these are bound to prove their pretended Authority by Miracles, if they will be believed by wise men that love salvation.

Reason 24.   Lastly, they teach but such like heresies, and take the like course, as many of the ancient heretics did . . . Presently, after the apostles' days, just such heretics as these arose and troubled the church. And they brought themselves to shame by their wickedness, folly and division, and God was still against them, and brought them to confusion . . . And shall we run ourselves into the fire, which hath consumed such heresies through former ages?

The following are extracts from the autobiographical writings of Richard Baxter:

In these times (especially since the Rump reign'd) sprang up five sects, at least, whose doctrines were almost the same, but they fell into several shapes and names: (1) the Vanists, (2) the Seekers, (3) the Ranters, (4) the Quakers, (5) the Behmenists . . .

. . . And that was the fourth sect, the Quakers, who were but the Ranters turned from horrid profaneness and blasphemy to a life of extreme austerity on the other side. Their doctrines were mostly the same with the Ranters. They make the light which every man hath within him to be his sufficient rule, and consequently the Scripture and ministry are set light by; they speak much for the dwelling working of the Spirit in us, but little of justification and the pardon of sin, and our reconciliation with God through Jesus Christ; they pretend their dependence on the Spirit's conduct, against set times of prayer and against sacraments, and against their due esteem of Scripture and ministry; they will not have the Scripture called the Word of God; their principal zeal lieth in railing at the ministers as hirelings, deceivers, false prophets, etc., and in refusing to swear before a magistrate, or to put off their hat to any, or to say 'You' instead of 'Thou' or 'Thee', which are their words to all . . . Many Franciscan friars and other Papists have been proved to be disguised speakers in their assemblies, and to be among them, and it's like are the very soul of all these horrible delusions. But of late one William Penn is become their leader, and would reform the sect and set up a kind of ministry among them.

[Referring to the period of persecution beginning in 1663]

And here the fanatics called Quakers did greatly relieve the sober people for a time; for they were so resolute, and gloried in their constancy and sufferings, that they assembled openly (at the Bull and Mouth near Aldersgate) and were dragged away daily to the common jail; And yet desisted not, but the rest came the next day nevertheless. So that the jail in Newgate was filled with them. Abundance of them died in prison, and yet they continued their assemblies still. And the poor deluded souls would sometimes meet only to sit in silence (when, as they said, the Spirit did not speak). And it was a great question whether this silence was a 'religious exercise not allowed by the liturgy', etc. And once upon some such reasons as these, when they were tried at the sessions in order to a banishment, the jury acquitted them, but were grievously threatened for it. After that another jury did acquit them, and some of them were fined and imprisoned for it. But thus the Quakers so employed Sir R.B. and the other searchers and prosecutors, that they had the less leisure to look after the meetings of soberer men, which was much to their present ease . . .

But many honest people were led to depart too far from the parish assemblies, and from charity and unity itself . . . Yea, many turned Quakers, because the Quakers kept their meetings openly, and went to prison for it cheerfully.

CHAPTER II

The Eighteenth Century

RICHARD GOUGH'S 'ANTIQUITIES AND MEMOIRS OF MYDDLE', written between 1700 and 1706, is an idiosyncratic collection of stories about people in a Shropshire village, as remembered by him or his informants. Here he says something about a temporary Quaker:

Elizabeth [Wolph] was marryed to one Edward Owen, a servant in Myddle. Arthur Owen, a taylor, who lives at Myddle town's end next the hill, is a son by that match. After the death of Edward Owen, shee was marryed to one Richard Clarke, of whom there is many remarkeable [*sic*] things to bee spoaken.

> Aude aliquid brevibus gyaris et carceris dignum
> Si vis esse aliquis. – Juvenal

> Do something that deserves the gallows,
> Or gaol, at least, if thou'lt be famous.

This Richard Clarke was the son of Richard Clarke, of myddle Wood. Hee was naturally ingeniouse. Hee had a smooth way of flattering discourse, and was a perfect master of the art of dissembling. He was listed for a soldier on the Parliament side in Wem, while hee was yett but a mere boy. There was nothing of manhood or valor in him, and yett hee was serviceable to the officers of that Garrison by carrying of letters to theire friends and correspondents that were in Garrisons of the adverse party. Hee had an old ragged coate on purpose which hee would putt on, and goe as a beggar boy. Hee carryed a short stick, such as boys call, a dog staffe. There was a hole boared in the end of it, and there the letters were putt, and a pegge after them, and that end hee putt in the dyrt. If hee mett with soldiers, hee would throw his sticke att birds, soe that it might goe over the hedge, and then goe over to fetch it. When hee came to the Garrison, hee wouald begg from doore to doore, and consort himselfe with beggars untill hee came to the place where hee was to deliver his letter. When a maid came to the doore, hee would desyre to speak to the Master, from a friend. When the Master came, hee would give him his sticke, and goe to cleane the stable untill the master brought his sticke, and then returne begging as beefore. After the warrs, hee marryed a wife that lived beyond Ellesmeare, her maiden name was Phillips. She was very thick of hearing, but yett shee was a comely woman, and had a portion in money, which Clarke quickly spent, for hee was a very drunken fellow if hee could gett money to spend. After hee had spent his wife's portion, hee came to Newton on the Hill, in a little house there under Mr. Gittin's and there hee sett up a trade of making spinning wheeles. He was not putt apprentice to any trade, and yett hee was very ingeniouse in workeing att any handycraft trade. Hee had a lytle smyth's forge, in which hee made his owne tooles, and likewise knives and other small things of iron. Hee had severall children by his first wife. The eldest hee named Jonathan, who now lives in Wem, and is as ingeniouse att working as his father, and as thicke of hearing as his mother. This Richard Clarke, after the death of his first wife, marryed Anne Onslow, of Clive. Shee was descended of good parentage, and was a comely and good humoured woman. About this time that phanaticall, self-conceited sort of people called Quakers beegan to start up here and there in this country. 'Nimietas plus obest quam prodest.' This Clarke, merely out of designe, had a minde to join with these persons. Hee went to one Gefferyes, of Stanton, (who was a topping Quaker), who received this new proselyte very gladly, and entertained him all night very kindly. Hee came home the next day a perfect Quaker in appearance, and had gott theire canting way of discourse as readyly as if hee had been seven years apprentice.

> Cum optimis satiati sumus, varietas etiam ex
> vilioribus grata est. – Quintil.

This Clarke was for a while of some repute among the Quakers, till att last hee had borrowed severall sums of money among them, which, when they required, hee att first gave fayre promises, butt att last utterly refused, telling them hee was not able, and they were worse than divells if they sued him. Upon this, att a general meeting of the Quakers, hee was excommunicated. This Clarke, whilst hee was in favour with the Quakers, had sadly abused our Ministers with his scurrilouse language, calling them hirelings, dumb doggs, and Baal's Priests. Hee was once bound to the behaivour for saying the Protector was the Beast, and the Whore did ride him. When Clarke was cast off by the Quakers, hee thought the Protestants would not receive him, and therefore hee turned Papist, butt was not regarded by that party . . .

SPECTATOR No 132   **Wednesday, August 1, 1711**

Qui, aut tempus quid postulet non videt, aut plura loquitur, aut se ostentat, aut eorum quibuscum est rationem non habet, ineptus esse dicitur. TULL.

Having notified to my good friend sir ROGER that I should set out for London, the next day, his horses were ready at the appointed hour in the evening;

and, attended by one of his grooms, I arrived at the county town at twilight, in order to be ready for the stage-coach the day following. As soon as we arrived at the inn, the servant, who waited upon me, inquaired of the chamberlain in my hearing, what company he had for the coach? The fellow answered, Mrs Betty Arable, the great fortune, and the widow her mother; a recruiting officer (who took a place because they were to go); young squire Quickset her cousin (that her mother wished her to be married to); Ephraim the quaker, her guardian; and a gentleman that had studied himself dumb, from sir ROGER DE COVERLEY'S. I perceived by what he said of myself, that according to his office he dealt much intelligence; and doubted not but there was some foundation for his reports for the rest of the company, as well as for the whimsical account he gave of me. The next morning at daybreak we were all called; and I, who know my own natural shyness, and endeavour to be as little liable to be disputed with as possible, dressed immediately, that I might make no one wait. The first preparation for our setting out was, that the captain's half-pike was placed near the coachman, and a drum behind the coach. In the mean time the drummer, the captain's equipage, was very loud, that none of the captain's things should be placed so as to be spoiled; upon which his cloak-bag was fixed in the seat of the coach; and the captain himself, according to a frequent, though invidious behaviour of military men, ordered his man to look sharp, that none but one of the ladies should have the place he had taken fronting to the coach-box.

We were in some little time fixed in our seats, and sat with that dislike which people not too good-natured usually conceive of each other at first sight. The coach jumbled us insensibly into some sort of familiarity; and we had not moved about two miles when the widow asked the captain what success he had had in his recruiting? The officer, with a frankness he believed very graceful, told her, 'That indeed he had but very little luck, and had suffered much by desertion, therefore should be glad to end his warfare in the service of her or her fair daughter. In a word, continued he, I am a soldier, and to be plain is my character: You see me, young, sound, and impudent: take me yourself, widow, or give me to her, I will be wholly at your disposal. I am a soldier of fortune, ha!' This was followed by a vain laugh of his own and a deep silence of all the rest of the company. I had nothing left for it but to fall fast asleep, which I did with all speed. 'Come,' said he, 'resolve upon it, we will make a wedding at the next town; we will make this pleasant companion who is fallen asleep, to be the brideman, and' (giving the quaker a clap on the knee) he concluded, 'This sly saint, who, I'll warrant, understands what's what as well as you or I, widow, shall give the bride as father.' The quaker, who happened to be a man of smartness, answered, 'Friend, I take it in good part that thou hast given me the authority of a father over this comely and virtuous child; and I must assure thee, that if I have the giving her, I shall not bestow her on thee. Thy mirth, friend, savoureth of folly: Thou art a person of a light mind; thy drum is a type of thee, it soundeth because it is empty. Verily, it is not from thy fullness, but thy emptiness that thou hast spoken this day. Friend, friend, we have hired this coach in partnership with thee, to carry us to the great city; we cannot go any other way. This worthy mother must hear thee, if thou wilt needs utter thy follies; we cannot help it, friend, I say: If thou wilt we must hear thee; but, if thou wert a man of understanding, thou wouldst not take advantage of thy courageous countenance to abash us children of peace. Thou art, thou sayest, a soldier; give quarter to us, who cannot resist thee. Why didst thou fleer* at our friend, who feigned himself asleep? He said nothing; but how doest thou know what he containeth? If thou speakest improper things in the hearing of this virtuous young virgin, consider it as an outrage against a distressed person that cannot get from thee: To speak indiscreetly what we are obliged to hear, by being hasped up with thee in this public vehicle, is in some degree assaulting on the high road.'

Here Ephraim paused, and the captain with a happy and uncommon impudence (which can be convicted and support itself at the same time) cries, 'Faith, friend, I thank thee; I should have been a little impertinent if thou hadst not reprimanded me. Come, thou art, I see, a smoky old fellow, and I'll be very. orderly the ensuing part of my journey. I was going to give myself airs, but, ladies, I'll beg pardon.'

The captain was so little out of humour, and our company was so far from being soured by this little ruffle, that Ephraim and he took a particular delight in being agreeable to each other for the future; and assumed their different provinces in the conduct of the company. Our reckonings, apartments and accommodation, fell under Ephraim: and the captain looked to all disputes upon the road, as the good behaviour of our coachman, and the right we had of taking place as going to London of all vehicles coming from thence. The occurences we met with were ordinary, and very little happened which could entertain by the relation of them: But when I considered the company we were in, I took it for no small good fortune that the whole journey was not spent in impertinencies, which to the one part of us might be an entertainment, to the other a suffering. What therefore Ephraim said when he were almost arrived at London, had to me the air not only of good understanding and good breeding. Upon the young lady's expressing her satisfaction in the journey, and declaring how delightful it had been to her, Ephraim delivered himself as follows: 'There is no ordinary part of human life which expresseth so much a good mind, and a right inward man, as his behaviour upon meeting with strangers, especially such as may seem the most unsuitable companions to him: Such a man, when he falleth in the way with persons of simplicity and innocence, however knowing he may be in the ways of men, will not vaunt himself thereof; but will rather hide his superiority to them, that he may not be painful unto them. My good friend, (continued he, turning to the officer) thee and I are to part by and by, and peradventure we may never meet again: But be advised by a plain man; modes and apparel are but trifles to the real man, therefore do not think such a man as thyself terrible for thy garb, nor such a man as me contemptible for mine. When two such as thee and I meet, with affections such as we ought to have towards each other, thou shouldest rejoice to see my peaceable demeanour, and I should be glad to see thy strength and ability to protect me in it.'

*to mock

16

Friday, December 10, 1714

I had occasion to go a few miles out of town, some days since, in a stagecoach, where I had for my fellow-travellers a dirty beau, and a pretty Quaker woman. . . . the pretty Quaker appeared in all the elegance of cleanliness. Not a speck was to be found on her. A clear, clean oval face, just edged about with little thin plaits of the purest cambrick, received great advantage from the shade of her black hood; as did the whiteness of her arms from that sober coloured stuff, in which she had cloathed her self. The plainness of her dress was very well suited to the simplicity of her phrases; all which put together, though they could not give me a great opinion of her religion, they did of her innocence.

Richard Steele (1672-1729)

The Fair Quakers: A Poem (1713)

The first edition of THE FAIR QUAKERS: A POEM *was published anonymously in 1713. An answering tract,* REMARKS ON A POEM, INTITULED, THE FAIR QUAKERS, *was published in 1714 in the form of a prose dialogue; records show that this was written by Josiah Martin, a Friend and member of Peel Meeting, London. A second and last edition of* THE FAIR QUAKERS *appeared in 1715, this time giving the author's name,* John Bingley, *and including a new poem purporting to be an elegy on his death from unrequited love. A brief extract from the original 376 lines of the poem gives some idea of its style:*[1]

The Fair Quakers: A Poem

(by John Bingley)

LONDON: Printed for J. Morphew, near Stationers' Hall. MDCCXIII.

The Publisher to the Reader.

I am very well acquainted that the excuses of a friend's importunity, or his stealing a copy, or its having unadvisedly been distributed, and so committed privately to the press, and the like, are so common and threadbare, that they are grown a standing jest: yet, . . . this is really the case . . . For the truth is, I saw and was pleased with the piece, which I found . . . to be easy, just, and entirely novel. For which reason I resolved without his [i.e. the author's] knowledge (whose consent I was sure never to obtain) to thrust it into the press: which is the main reason why you now find it made public . . . So, Reader, I leave it with you, and wish you as much pleasure in perusing it as I had.

> Well, unknown youth, hast thou the Friends expressed,
> And thy Fair Quakers like themselves hast dressed:
> Moving and soft, and gaily innocent;
> Without excess, yet full of ornament.
> Of youthful virtue thus proceed to write,
> And by example as by verse invite.
> With innocence and beauty grace your strains,
> The listening isle shall bless your tuneful pains:
> Virtue resume her sway and vice retire,
> And O---d reign, while thus she does inspire
> The Friendly muse, and guide the Quaker lyre.

R.S. [Richard Steele?]

The Fair Quakers: A Poem

> Aid, sacred nymphs of the Pierian spring!
> Whilst I no vulgar theme attempt to sing.
> And Phoebus, tuneful God, my breast inspire,
> Expand my soul with thy celestial fire,
> Conduct those numbers, and direct those lays
> Which I now dedicate to Beauty's praise.
> Thy kind assistance, too, soft God of Love,
> To me vouchsafe, thy influence let me prove.
> Virgins from thee derive their various charms . . .
> Instruct me then their beauties to rehearse,   13
> And let their names immortalise my verse . . .
> Fair O---d now too strongly does attest   19
> Thy potent sway, and wounds my suffering breast:
> Thy godhead I confess, oh! move the Fair
> To hear and be propitious to my prayer . . .
>
> Begin, auspicious muse, the pleasing song,   25
> Fired with new beauties as thou goest along.
> See lovely B---rs first in sight appears,
> A blooming virgin in her prime of years; [=youthfulness]

Graceful her shape, delightful is her mien;
An unaffected smile, an air serene
Adorn her face, where growing charms are seen . . .

Ma---n with conquering charms the soul commands,   36
And captive leads the heart in willing hands;
The sparkling lustre of her radiant eyes
The lover's breast invades with sweet surprise . . .

Behold, a younger Ma---n comes in sight,   48
Who shortly will shine forth with wondrous light:
Her budding charms uncommon lustre spread,
And beaming glories crown her youthful head . . .

Nor, W---n, shall thy worth unsung remain   55
Misfortunes never shall thy lustre stain;
Thy pleasing beauties cheer the ravished sight,
And soothe the senses with a strange delight;
Each sundry charm adversity refines,
Like diamonds set in jet thy virtue shines.

Young H---s appears, all innocently gay,
Driving from every breast despair away;
So affable the Fair, so soft and kind,
She frees from gloomy cares the lover's mind . . .

F---n a fatal splendour darts abroad,   71
Which comet-like, sure ruin does forebode;
Her lovers trembling view her, and admire
The glittering cause of such destructive fire . . .

Engaging M---re appears with artless grace,   83
A thousand blooming charms adorn her face . . .

Next I admire fair W---r's name,   87
W---r whose wit deserves immortal fame: . . .
With which resplendent beauty does combine   95
To make the charming maid conspicuous shine.

Fair P---m next behold, serenely gay,
Pleasing as summer's shades and mild as May:
As roses in their vernal bloom appear,

To sight and smell delicious, sweet and fair,
Some with their crimson blush delight the view,
And others with their native snowy hue;
In F---m's cheeks these opposites unite,
The blushing crimson and the snowy white . . . .

And Oh! ye powers! whate'er my lot may prove,
On her shower all your blessings from above:
Still may her hours dance on with shining joy,
Free from corroding grief's unkind alloy.
That when her native sky she shall ascend,
And every doubt or sorrow shall have end,
The charmer, in that perfect state, may know
Blessings above more great than those she left below.

The following is a further extract from QUAKERS OBSERVED IN PROSE AND VERSE,
included in A QUAKER MISCELLANY FOR EDWARD MILLIGAN *(see above, page 7).*

'The Quaker Song' in Thomas D'Urfey's PILLS TO PURGE MELANCHOLY
(1719-1720) mocks Friends' ideals of purity and conscience by proposing hypocritical attitudes and motives of lustfulness. In five eight line stanzas D'Urfey
relates a Quaker seduction, justified by following the leading of the spirit between
'a Holy Sister' and 'a Friend and Brother!' (The terms 'Sister' and 'Brother' are
not to be taken literally; the imputation is not one of incest.) The result of the
seduction is, as one might expect, a pregnancy:

> But when the time was come,
>   That she was to be laid;
> It was not a very great Crime,
>   Committed by her they said:
> 'Cause they did know, and she did show,
>   'Twas done by a Friend and a Brother,
> But a very great Sin they said it had been,
>   If it had been done by another.

A second song in PILLS TO PURGE MELANCHOLY, 'The Penurious Quaker
or, the High Priz'd Harlot', takes Quaker lechery for granted, but adds to it a
jibe at the Quaker's stinginess in paying for the whore's services. It also mocks
the Quaker's reputation for truthfulness in the words put into his mouth:

I cannot like the Wicked say,
   I love thee and Adore thee,
And therefore thou wilt make me pay,
   So here is sixpence for thee.

On Barclay's Apology for the Quakers

Matthew Green (1696-1737)

These sheets primeval doctrines yield,
Where revelation is revealed:
Soul-phlegm from literal feeding bred,
Systems lethargic to the head,
They purge and leave a diet thin,
That turns to gospel chyle★ within.
Truth sublimate may here be seen
Extracted from the parts terrene.†
In these is shown how men obtain
What of Prometheus poets faign:
To scripture-plainness dress is brought
And speech, apparel to the thought.
They hiss from instinct at red coats,
And war, whose work is cutting throats,
Forbid, and press the law of love,
Breathing the spirit of the dove.
Lucrative doctrines they detest,
As manufactured by the priest:
And throw down turnpikes, where we pay
For stuff which never mends the way;
And tithes, a Jewish tax, reduce,
And frank the gospel for our use.
They sable standing armies break,
But the militia useful make;
Since all unhired may preach and pray,

★ A thin whitish fluid: lymph
† of the earth: mundane

21

Taught by these rules as well as they,
Rules, which, when truths themselves reveal,
Bid us to follow what we feel.

The world can't hear the small still voice,
Such is its bustle and its noise;
Reason the proclamation reads,
But not one note passion heeds.
Wealth, honour, power and graces are,
Which here below our homage share:
They, if one votary they find
To mistress more divine inclined,
In truth's pursuit to cause delay
Throw golden apples in his way.

Place me, O heav'n in some retreat,
There let the serious death-watch beat,
There let me self in silence shun,
To feel thy will, which should be done.

Then comes the spirit to our hut
When fast the senses' doors are shut;
For so divine and pure a guest
The emptiest rooms are furnished best.

O Contemplation! air serene,
From damps of sense, and fogs of spleen!
Pure mount of thought! thrice holy ground,
Where grace, when waited for, is found.

Here 'tis the soul feels sudden youth,
And meek, exulting, virgin Truth;
Here, like a breeze of gentlest kind,
Impulses rustle through the mind;
Here shines that light with glowing face,
The fuse divine that kindles grace,
Which, if we trim our lamps, will last
Till darkened by the dying past,
And then goes out at end of night,
Extinguished by superior light.

Ah me! the heats and colds of life,
Pleasures and Pain's eternal strife,
Breed stormy passions which, confined,
Shake, like th' Aeolian cave, the mind,
And raise despair my lamp can last,
Placed where they drive their furious blast.

False eloquence, big empty sound,
Like showers that rush upon the ground,
Little beneath the surface goes,

All streams along and muddy flows.
This sinks and swells the buried grain,
And fructifies like southern rain.

His art, well hid in mild discourse,
Exerts persuasions winning force,
And nervates★ so the good design,
That king Agrippa's cause is mine.

Well natured, happy shade, forgive!
Like you I think, but cannot live.
Thy scheme requires the world's contempt,
That, from dependence life exempt,
And constitution framed so strong,
This world's worst climate cannot wrong.
Not such my lot, not fortune's brat,
I live by putting off the hat,
Compelled by station every hour
To bow to images of power,
And, in life's busy scenes immersed,
See better things and do the worst.

Eloquent Want, whose reasons sway,
And make ten thousand truths give way,
While I your scheme with pleasure trace,
Draws near and stares me in the face.
'Consider well your state,' she cries,
'Like others kneel, that you may rise;
'Hold doctrines, by no scruple vexed,
'To which preferment is annexed,
'Nor madly prove, where all depends,
'Idolatry upon your friends.
'See how you like my rueful face;
'Such you must wear, if out of place.
'Cracked is your brain to turn recluse
'Without one farthing out at use.
'They who have lands and safe bank-stock,
'With faith so founded on a rock,
'May give a rich invention ease,
'And construe scripture how they please.'

The honoured prophet, that of old
Used heav'n's high counsels to unfold,
Did, more than courier angels, greet
The crows, that brought him bread and meat.

★ strengthens

23

A JOURNAL OF THE PLAGUE YEAR – Daniel Defoe (1661?-1731)

In his Introduction to this 1884 edition Henry Morley pointed out that Daniel Defoe was apparently only four years old in the Plague year of 1665. The JOURNAL reads as the narrative of an eye-witness, but it is in fact a brilliant piece of reconstruction. The burial-ground to which Defore refers was probably Bunhill Fields, the dissenting burial-ground:

Another run about Naked, except a pair of Drawers about his Waist, crying Day and Night; like a Man that Josephus mentions, who cry'd, woe to Jerusalem! a little before the Destruction of that City: So this poor naked Creature cry'd, 'O! the Great, and the Dreadful God!' and said no more, but repeated those Words continuously, with a Voice and Countenance full of horror, a swift Pace, that I ever cou'd hear of. I met this poor Creature several Times in the Streets, and would have spoke to him, but he would not enter into Speech with me, or any one else; but held on his dismal Cries continuously . . . (pp 34-35)

I should have mentioned, that the Quakers had at that time also a burying Ground, set apart to their Use, and which they still make use of, and they had also a particular death Cart to fetch their Dead from their Houses; and the famous Solomon Eagle, who, as I mentioned before, had predicted the Plague as a Judgment, and run nak'd thro' the Street, telling the People, that it was come upon them, to punish them for their Sins, had his own Wife died the very next Day of the Plague, and was carried one of the first in the Quakers death Cart, to their new burying Ground . . . (p 296)

MOLL FLANDERS and ROXANA – Daniel Defoe

These two novels by Daniel Defoe, MOLL FLANDERS published in 1721 and ROXANA published in 1724, provide an interesting contrast to the popular view of Quakers at that time as proud and lecherous hypocrites. In each of the novels the Quaker is portrayed as helpful, kind and honest, a thoroughly good man or woman, against the tawdry anti-heroines of the books. Defoe had clearly met Quakers, knew them well and liked what he knew and sets them up as examples against the licentiousness of the age.

Moll Flanders

In this novel Moll Flanders and her husband have arrived in America and have decided to settle in Carolina. They hear of a ship going there from Maryland, across Chesapeake Bay and after five days' sailing they arrive at a place called Philip's Point. There they learn that the ship for Carolina sailed two days before they arrived:

We immediately went on shore, but found no conveniences just at that place, either for our being on shore, or preserving our goods on shore, but was directed by a very honest quaker, who we found there, to go to a place about sixty miles east; that is to say, nearer the mouth of the bay, where he said he lived, and where we should be accommodated, either to plant, or to wait for any other place to plant in that might be more convenient; and he invited us with so much kindness that we agreed to go, and the quaker himself went with us.

Here we bought us two servants, viz., an English woman-servant, just come on shore from a ship from Liverpool, and a negro man-servant, things absolutely necessary for all people that pretended to settle in that country. This honest quaker was very helpful to us, and when we came to the place that he proposed, found us out a convenient storehouse for our goods, and lodging for ourselves and servants; and about two months, or thereabouts, afterwards, by his direction, we took up a large piece of land from the government of that country, in order to form our plantation, and so we laid the thoughts of going to Carolina wholly aside, having been very well received here, and accommodated with a lodging till we could prepare things, and have land enough cured, and materials provided for building us a house, all which we managed by the direction of the quaker . . . (p 272)

Roxana, or the Fortunate Mistress

This novel is set in the reign of Charles II and is the history of a whore. After many adventures she begins to reflect seriously on her way of life and determines to leave the locality where she is known, to begin a new life in a fresh neighbourhood. Her maid Amy finds her a house in the Minories in London:

Amy agreed for a good handsome price, because she was resolved I should be used well, so she bargained to give her [the mistress of the house] £35 for the half-year, and £50 if we took a maid, leaving that to my choice; and that we might be satisfied we should meet with nothing very gay, the people were Quakers, and I liked them the better.

I was so pleased, that I resolved to go with Amy the next day to see the lodgings, and to see the woman of the house, and see how I liked them, but if I was pleased with the general, I was much more pleased with the particulars; for the gentlewoman, I must call her so, though she was a Quaker, was a most courteous, obliging, mannerly person; perfectly well-bred, and perfectly well-humoured, and, in short, which was worth all, so grave, and yet so pleasant and so merry, that 'tis scarce possible for me to express how I was pleased and delighted with her company; and particularly, I was so pleased that I would go away no more; so I e'en took up my lodging there the very first night . . . (p 185)

This good (though unhappy) Quaker had the misfortune to have had a bad husband, and he was gone beyond sea, she had a good house, and well-furnished, and had some jointure of her own estate, which supported her and her children, so that she did not want; but she was not at all above such a help as my being there was to her; so she was as glad of me as I was of her . . . (p 186)

Roxana, as it will appear for her own ends, plans to make a friend of the Quaker and makes her a present of a piece of very fine new holland cloth, against which she protests:

What dost thou mean? says she; indeed I cannot have the face to accept so fine a present as this; adding, 'tis fit for thy own use, but 'tis above my wear, indeed. I thought she had meant she must not wear it so fine, because she was a Quaker; so I returned, Why, do not you Quakers wear fine linen neither? Yes, says she, we wear fine linen when we can afford it, but this is too good for me. However, I made her take it, and she was very thankful too; but my end was answered another way, for by this I engaged her so that as I found her a woman of understanding, and of honesty too, I might, upon any occasion, have a confidence in her, which was, indeed, what I very much wanted . . . (p 187)

But Roxana's motives are, as ever, devious and in the episode of the coach Defoe shows the Quaker's integrity beginning to be assailed by her lack of honesty:

By accustoming myself to converse with her, I had not only learned to dress like a Quaker, but so used myself to 'thee' and 'thou', that I talked like a Quaker too, as readily and naturally as if I had been born among them; and, in a word, I passed for a Quaker among all people that did not know me. I went but little abroad, but I had been so used to a coach, that I knew not how well to go without one; besides, I thought it would be a farther disguise to me, so I told my Quaker friend one day, that I thought I lived too close, that I wanted air; she proposed taking a hackney-coach sometimes, or a boat; but I told her I had always had a coach of my own till now, and I could find in my heart to have one again.

She seemed to think it strange at first, considering how close I lived, but had nothing to say when she found I did not value the expense; so, in short, I resolved I would have a coach. When we came to talk of equipages, she extolled the having all things plain. I said so too; so I left it to her direction and a coach-maker was sent for, and he provided me a plain coach, no gilding or painting, lined with a light grey cloth, and my coachman had a coat of the same, and no lace on his hat.

When all was ready, I dressed myself in the dress I had bought of her, and said, Come, I'll be a Quaker today and you and I'll go abroad; which we did, and there was not a Quaker in the town looked less like a counterfeit than I did. But all this was my particular plot, to be more completely concealed, and that I might depend upon being not known, and yet need not be confined like a prisoner, and be always in fear; so that all the rest was grimace . . . (pp 187-188)

26

Roxana's past catches up with her when a Dutch merchant whom she had known in her old life discovers where she is living and seeks her out. She does not wish to see him, but the Quaker, who is ignorant of her past life, persuades her to allow him to visit her. When Roxana finally marries the Dutch merchant the Quaker gives them a celebratory meal and looks after them for a week.

There is a point in the story when the Quaker's behaviour seems a little out of keeping with her religious profession; she shows herself as very experienced in amorous adventures (p 196). She also appears at times very gullible. But she has an important part to play in the development of the plot and on the whole Defoe presents her as a staunch friend and a good woman, in complete contrast to Roxana's lies, deviousness and sexual adventures.

CAPTAIN SINGLETON, an earlier novel published in 1720, shows Defoe portraying a different kind of Quaker in the character of the ship's surgeon William Walters, who seems to compromise with all the principles Quakers held most dear.

Captain Singleton of the title was born a gentleman, but took to the sea and eventually became Cap'n Bob of a pirate ship. When he and his crew capture a sloop, the Quaker surgeon, William Walters, described as '"a common fellow" indeed , a man of very good sense and an excellent surgeon,' is seized and taken aboard the pirate ship, but he insists that the master of the sloop should sign a certificate to the effect that he and his case of instruments were taken away by main force. He will not have it thought that he would willingly have taken to piracy, although he remains with Cap'n Bob throughout the book. He promises Cap'n Bob to be as useful as he can, though he adds the rider – 'but thou knowest it is not my business to meddle when thou art to fight'. But William is not above accepting his share of any prize money and the captain realises that he has made sure that 'If we were taken, we were sure to be hanged, and he was sure to escape, and he knew it well enough'.

Throughout the story William shows he is more cunning and calculating than Cap'n Bob and his crew and so his advice, which he is not above giving, is frequently followed. He is cool and resourceful under fire – 'there was William as composed, and in as perfect tranquillity as to danger as if he had been over a bowl of punch'. He does in fact meddle in the fight, advising Cap'n Bob to order his men to board a partially crippled vessel with the words – '"Friend," says he very calmly, "what dost thou mean? Why dost thou not visit thy neighbour in the ship, the door being open for thee?"'

William is also shown as giving advice to the pirates, in suggesting that they would be better to attack only merchant shipping, although occasionally Defoe allows him to have 'some quakerly quibble or other'. But it is clear that he was not above taking and trading in slaves. When the pirates arrive off the coast of Brazil William trades all the negroes the pirates had captured with planters and 'in less than 5 weeks he had sold all his negroes'. In return for some help a planter gives him a negro girl for his wife. William is made captain of a sloop (which he obtained in exchange for the slaves) on condition that he remains with the pirates. He does, however, prevail upon Cap'n Bob to save some captured Dutchmen from being thrown overboard.

Although Defoe presents William as being willing to abandon his peace-loving principles by profitting from piracy he points out that William was 'always for doing . . . business without fighting' *in that he is shown as persuading Cap'n Bob to turn to trading in the Dutch East Indies. But William is also shown as ready to abandon his principles when necessary and, when the pirates were besieging some* 'barbarous natives' *holed up in a tree-fort,* 'William the quaker, whose curiosity led him to go among the rest, proposed that they should make a ladder, and get upon the top, and then throw wild-fire into the tree to smoke them out'. *He then advises boring holes in the tree and filling them with gunpowder and* 'desired that 3 men might be given him with hand-grenades and he promised to go first, and boldly he did so; for William, to give him his due, had the heart of a lion'. *Finally, after his successful career as a pirate and trader, the evil of his ways comes home to William and with tears in his eyes he begs Cap'n Bob to repent. The two abandon piracy and settle on shore. As a kind of reckoning with God they send thousands of pounds to William's sister, who has been left a widow with four children. When they eventually return to England Cap'n Bob marries William's sister and here Defoe's irony becomes apparent. The gesture of renunciation is made, but in such a way that they can continue to enjoy their ill-gotten gains.*

In contrasting the portrayal of William with that of Quakers in the two later novels Defoe's intention becomes clear. A strand running through all three books is the helpfulness of the Quakers: however much they appear to compromise with their principles they are fundamentally good. William, although he would rather not fight, cannot refrain from helping the pirates to manage their affairs better, even to the extent of showing them what to do to achieve a victory over their enemies (a contributory reason for this may of course be that Defoe desires to show his hero as having greater intelligence and being braver and more powerful than the pirates). But in MOLL FLANDERS *the Quaker Moll meets goes to great lengths to help her and her husband settle in Maryland and in* ROXANA *the Quaker lady is there, at every turn and twist of the first half of the story, to befriend and help the heroine. Defoe clearly shares the prevailing view that Quakers would abandon their principles if the situation demanded. In choosing to set Quakers against the great depths of wickedness and licentiousness he found in his own time he obviously found them to be capable of genuine goodness.*

Voltaire *(1694-1778) was the name by which* Francois Marie Arouet, *who was born in Paris, was generally known. He came to England in 1726 and the three years he spent here until he returned to France in 1729 provided the basis for his* LETTRES PHILOSOPHIQUE, *reflections on various aspects of English life. Of Quakerism he is critical but not unkind.* LETTER 1 *is appreciative of Friends, although not entirely in agreement with them; he fails in* LETTER 2 *to be impressed by a Quaker meeting for worship, but he reports the explanation he was given without ridicule. In* LETTER 3 *he is not exactly charitable to George Fox, but to a man of his social background and intellectual attainments Fox would deserve scorn as illiterate and Quaker customs appear merely foolish. But even in* LETTER 3 *Voltaire is amazed (or admiring) when he reads Robert Barclay's* 'EPISTLE' *to Charles II and* LETTER 4 *is not lacking in praise for William Penn:*

LETTER 1: I was of the opinion, that the doctrine and history of so extraordinary a people, were worthy the attention of the curious. To acquaint myself with them, I made a visit to one of the most eminent Quakers in England, who after having traded thirty years, had the wisdom to prescribe limits to his fortune and to his desires, and was settled in a little solitude not far from London. Being come into it, I perceiv'd a small, but regularly built house, vastly neat, but without the least pomp of furniture. The Quaker who own'd it, was a hale ruddy complexion'd old man, who had never been afflicted with sickness because he had always been insensible to passions, and a perfect stranger to intemperance. I never in my life saw a more noble or more engaging aspect than his. He was dress'd like those of his persuasion, in a plain coat, without pleats in the sides, or buttons on the pockets and sleeves; and had on a beaver, the brims of which were horizontal, like those of our clergy. He did not uncover himself when I appear'd, and advanc'd towards me without stooping his body; but there appear'd more politeness in the open, humane air of his countenance, than in the custom of drawing one leg behind the other, and taking that from the head, which is made to cover it. Friend, says he to me, I perceive thou art a stranger, but if I can do anything for thee, only tell me. Sir, says I to him, bending forwards, and advancing as is usual with us, one leg towards him, I flatter myself that my just curiosity will not give you the least offence, and then you'll do me the honour to inform me of the particulars of your religion. The people of thy country, replied the Quaker, are too full of their bows and compliments, but I never met with one of them who had so much curiosity as thy self. Come in, and let us dine together first. I still continued to make some very unseasonable ceremonies, it not being easy to disengage one's self at once from habits we have been long us'd to; and after taking part of a frugal meal, which began and ended with a prayer to God, I began to question my courteous host. I open'd with that which good Catholicks have more than once made to Huguenots. My dear sir, says I, were you ever baptiz'd? I never was, replied the Quaker, nor any of my brethren. Zouns, says I to him, you are not a Christian then. Friend, replies the old man in a soft tone of voice, swear not; we are Christians, and endeavour to be good Christians, but we are not of opinion, that the sprinkling of water on a child's head makes him a Christian. Heavens! says I, shock'd at his impiety, you have then forgot that Christ was baptiz'd by St. John. Friend, replies the mild Quaker once again, swear not. Christ indeed was baptiz'd by John, but in himself never baptiz'd any one. We are disciples of Christ, not of John. I pitied very much the sincerity of my worthy Quaker, and was absolutely forcing him to get himself christned [*sic*]. Were

29

that all, replied he very gravely, we would submit chearfully to baptism, purely in compliance with thy weakness, for we don't condemn any person who uses it; but then we think that those who profess a religion of so holy, so spiritual a nature as that of Christ, ought to abstain to the utmost of their power from the Jewish ceremonies. O unaccountable! says I, what! baptism a Jewish ceremony? Yes, my friend says he, so truly Jewish, that a great many Jews use the baptism of John to this day. Look into ancient authors, and thou wilt find that John only reviv'd this practice; and that it had been us'd by the Hebrews, long before his time, in like manner as the Mahometans imitated the Ishmaelites in their pilgrimage to Mecca. Jesus indeed submitted to the baptism of John, as he had suffer'd himself to be circumcis'd, but circumcision and the washing of water ought to be abolished by the baptism of Christ, that baptism of the spirit, that absolution of the soul, which is the salvation of mankind. Thus the forerunner said, I indeed baptize you with water unto repentance; but he that cometh after me, is mightier than I, whose shoes I am not worthy to bear: he shall baptize you with the Holy Ghost and with fire. Likewise Paul, the great apostle of the Gentiles, writes as follows to the Corinthians; *Christ sent me not to baptize but to preach the Gospel,* and indeed Paul never baptiz'd but two persons with water, and that very much against his inclinations. He circumcis'd his disciple Timothy, and the other disciples likewise circumcis'd all who were willing to submit to that carnal ordinance. But art thou circumcis'd, added he? I have not the honour to be so, says I. Well, friend, continues the Quaker, thou art a Christian without being circumcis'd, and I am one without being baptiz'd. Thus did this pious man make a wrong, but very specious application, of four or five texts of scriptures which seem'd to favour the tenets of his sect; but at the same time forgot very sincerely an hundred texts which made directly against them. I had more sense than to contest with him, since there is no possibility of convincing an enthusiast. A man shou'd never pretend to inform a lover of his mistress's faults, no more than one who is at law, of the badness of his cause; nor attempt to win over a fanatic by strength of reasoning. Accordingly I wav'd the subject . . .

LETTER 2: Voltaire is taken by his friend to a Quaker meeting:

. . . I was greatly surpriz'd to see him come the Sunday following, and take me with him to the Quaker's meeting. There are several of these in London, but that which he carried me to stands near the famous pillar call'd the monument. The brethren were already assembled at my entering with my guide. There might be about four hundred men and three hundred women in the meeting. The women hid their faces behind their fans, and the men were cover'd with their broad-brimm'd hats; all were seated, and the silence was universal. I past [*sic*] through them, but did not perceive so much as one lift up his eyes to look at me. This silence lasted a quarter of an hour, when at last one of them rose up, took off his hat, and after making a variety of wry faces, and groaning in a most lamentable manner, he partly from his nose, and partly from his mouth, threw out a strange confus'd jumble of words, (borrow'd as he imagin'd from the Gospel) which neither himself nor any of his hearers understood. When this distorter had ended his beautiful soliloquy, and that the stupid, but greatly edified congregation were separated, I ask'd my friend how it was possible for the judicious part of their assembly to suffer such a babbling. We are oblig'd, says he, to suffer it, because no one knows when a man rises up to hold forth, whether he will be mov'd by the spirit or by folly. In this doubt and uncertainty we listen patiently to every one, we even allow our women to hold forth; two or three of these are often inspir'd at one and the same time, and 'tis then that a most charming noise is heard from the Lord's house. You have then no priests, says I to him. No, no, friend, replies the Quaker, to our great happiness. Then opening one of the friend's books, as he call'd it, he read the following words in an emphatic tone: God forbid we should presume to ordain any one to receive the holy spirit on the Lord's day, to the prejudice of the rest of the brethren. Thanks to the almighty, we are the only people upon earth that have no priests. Wouldest thou deprive us of so happy a distinction? Why shou'd we abandon our babe to mercenary nurses, when we ourselves have milk enough for it? These mercenary creatures wou'd soon domineer in our houses, and destroy both the mother and the babe. God has said, freely you have receiv'd, freely give. Shall we after these words cheapen, as it were, the Gospel; sell the Holy Ghost, and make of an assembly of Christians a mere shop of traders. We don't pay a sett [*sic*] of men cloath'd in black, to assist our poor, to bury our dead, or to preach to the brethren; these offices are all of too tender a nature, for us ever to entrust them to others. But how is it possible for you, says I, with some warmth, to know whether your discourse is really inspir'd by the Almighty? Whosoever, says he, shall implore Christ to enlighten him, and shall publish the Gospel truths he may feel inwardly, such an one may be assur'd that he is inspir'd by the Lord. He then pour'd forth a numberless multitude of Scripture-texts, which prov'd, as he imagin'd, that there is no such thing as Christianity without an immediate revelation . . .

LETTER 3: This letter contains Voltaire's summary of early Quaker history, ending with Robert Barclay's dedicatory epistle to Charles II at the beginning of the APOLOGY. Barclay reminds Charles II of his own misfortunes and urges him not to play the part of an oppressor. Voltaire concludes that after this persecution of the Quakers ceased, which is of course incorrect.

LETTER 4: This is a very favourable account of William Penn and the founding of Pennsylvania, but Voltaire closes his LETTERS ON QUAKERS on a melancholy note: I am not able to guess what fate Quakerism may have in America, but I perceive it dwindles away daily in England. In all countries where liberty of conscience is allow'd, the establish'd religion will at last swallow up all the rest. Quakers are disqualified from being members of parliament; nor can they enjoy any post or preferment, because an oath must always be taken on these occasions, and they never swear. They are therefore reduc'd to the necessity of subsisting upon traffick. Their children, whom the industry of their parents has enrich'd, are desirous of enjoying honours, of wearing buttons and ruffles; and quite asham'd of being call'd Quaker, they become converts of the Church of England, merely to be in the fashion.

TOM JONES – Henry Fielding (1707-1754)

The Quaker who appears in this novel, first published in 1749, is portrayed as at first a kindly, well-meaning man who befriends Tom Jones on his way to Bristol. Tom has asked the way of two fellows who have only contrived to muddle him with their directions and the Quaker advises him to stay overnight in a nearby public house and to continue his journey by daylight. During his conversation with Tom Jones the Quaker reveals that his daughter has made a runaway marriage, to his great distress. In the father's condemnation of such folly Fielding presents what was probably a view of Quakers as concerned above all else with money, a view no doubt aggravated by jealousy of their increasing prosperity in business brought about by their honesty and integrity as traders; they could be trusted implicitly in an age when honest dealing was not always the rule. The Quaker as presented by Fielding is more concerned that his daughter shall have no further claim to his money than for her future happiness and he is only willing to befriend Tom Jones until he learns that Tom is 'a fellow of low birth and no future', one who cannot therefore merit his compassion or interest. In Fielding's insistence on his honesty and plainness there is more than a hint of irony, a suggestion that low birth and lack of money are as much an affront to him as to the wealthiest and most aristocratic of men. The extracts concerning him are as follows:

These two fellows had almost conquered the patience of Jones, when a plain well-looking man (who was indeed a Quaker) accosted him thus; 'Friend, I perceive thou has lost thy way; and if thou wilt take my advice, thou wilt not attempt to find it to-night. It is almost dark, and the road is difficult to hit; besides there have been several robberies committed lately between this and Bristol. Here is a very creditable house just by, where thou may'st find good entertainment for thyself and thy cattle till morning'. Jones, after a little persuasion, agreed to stay in this place 'till morning, and was conducted by his friend to the public-house.

The landlord, who was a very civil fellow, told Jones, 'he hoped he would excuse the badness of his accommodation: for that his wife was gone from home, and had locked up almost every thing, and carried the keys along with her'. Indeed, the fact was, that a favourite daughter of hers was just married, and gone, that morning, home with her husband; and that she and her mother together, had almost stript the poor man of all his goods, as well as money: for tho' he had several children, this daughter only, who was the mother's favourite, was the object of her consideration; and to the humour of this one child she would, with pleasure, have sacrificed all the rest, and her husband into the bargain.

Tho' Jones was very unfit for any kind of company, and would have preferred being alone, yet he could not resist the importunities of the honest Quaker; who was the more desirous of sitting with him, from having remarked the melancholy which appeared both in his countenance and behaviour; and which the poor Quaker thought his conversation might in some measure relieve.

After they had passed some time together, in such manner that my honest friend might have thought himself at one of his silent-meetings, the Quaker began to be moved by some spirit or other, probably that of curiosity; and said, 'Friend, I perceive some sad disaster hath befallen thee; but, pray be of comfort. Perhaps thou hast lost a friend. If so, thou must consider we are all mortal. And why should'st thou grieve, when thou knowest thy grief will do thy friend no good. We are all born to affliction. I myself have my sorrows as well as thee, and most probably greater sorrows. Tho' I have a clear estate of £100 a year, which is as much as I want, and I have a conscience, I thank the Lord, void of offence. My constitution is strong and sound, and there is no man can demand a debt of me, nor accuse me of an injury – yet, friend, I should be concerned to think thee as miserable as myself'.

Here the Quaker ended with a deep sigh; and Jones presently answered, 'I am very sorry, sir, for your unhappiness, whatever is the occasion of it'. 'Ah! friend,' replied the Quaker, 'my one only daughter is the occasion. One who was my greatest delight upon earth, and who within this week is run away from me, and is married against my consent. I had provided her a proper match, a sober man, and one of substance, but she, forsooth, would chuse for herself, and away she is gone with a young fellow not worth a groat. If she had been dead, as I suppose thy friend is, I should have been happy!' 'That is very strange, sir,' said Jones. 'Why, would it not be better for her to be dead, than to be a beggar?' replied the Quaker: 'for, as I told you, the fellow is nor worth a groat; and surely she cannot expect that I shall ever give her a shilling. No, as she hath married for love, let her live on love if she can; let her carry her love to market, and see whether any one will change it into silver, or even halfpence.' 'You know your own concerns best, sir,' said Jones. 'It must have been,' continued the Quaker, 'a long premeditated scheme to cheat me: for they have known one another from their infancy; and I have always preached to her against love – and told her a thousand times over it was all folly and wickedness. Nay, the cunning slut pretended to hearken to me, and to despise all wantonness of the flesh; and yet, at last, to break out at a window two pair of stairs: for I began, indeed, a little to suspect her, and had locked her up carefully, intending the next morning to have married her to my liking. But she disappointed me within a few hours, and escaped away to the lover of her own chusing, who lost no time; for they were married and bedded, all within an hour.

'But it shall be the worst hour's work for them both that ever they did, for they may starve, or beg, or steal together for me. I will never give either of them a farthing.' Here Jones starting up, cry'd, 'I really must be excused; I wish you would leave me'. 'Come, come, friend,' said the Quaker, 'don't give way to concern. You see there are other people miserable, besides yourself.' 'I see there are madmen and fools and villains in the world,' cries Jones – 'But let me give you a piece of advice; send for your daughter and son-in-law home, and don't be yourself the only cause of misery to one you pretend to love.' 'Send for her and her husband home!' cries the Quaker loudly, 'I would sooner send for the two greatest enemies I have in the world!' 'Well, go home yourself, or where you please,' said Jones: 'for I will sit no longer in such company.' 'Nay, friend,' answered the Quaker, 'I scorn to impose my company on any one.' He then offered to pull money from his pocket, but Jones pushed him with some violence out of the room.

The subject of the Quaker's discourse had so deeply affected Jones, that he stared very wildly all the time he was speaking. This the Quaker had observed, and this, added to the rest of his behaviour, inspired honest Broadbrim with a conceit, that his companion was, in reality, out of his senses. Instead of resenting the affront, therefore, the Quaker was moved with compassion for his unhappy circumstances; and having communicated his opinion to the landlord, he desired him to take great care of his guest, and to treat him with the highest civility.

'Indeed,' says the landlord, 'I shall use no such civility towards him: for it seems, for all his faced waistcoat there, he is no more a gentleman than myself; but a poor parish bastard bred up at a great squire's about 30 miles off, and now turned out of doors, (not for any good to be sure). I shall get him out of my house as soon as possible. If I do lose my reckoning, the first loss is always the best. It is not above a year ago that I lost a silver-spoon.'

'What dost thou talk of a parish bastard, Robin?' answered the Quaker. 'Thou has certainly been mistaken in thy man.'

'Not at all,' replied Robin, 'the guide, who knows him very well, told it me.' For, indeed, the guide had no sooner taken his place at the kitchen-fire, than he acquainted the whole company with all he knew, or had ever heard concerning Jones.

The Quaker was no sooner assured by this fellow of the birth and low fortune of Jones, than all compassion for him vanished; and the honest, plain man went home fired with no less indignation than a duke would have felt at receiving an affront from such a person.

David Hume, who was born in Edinburgh in 1711, was one of the two great philosophers of the 18th-century Age of Enlightenment. He held the religious sects which came into existence during the Commonwealth period to be fanatical in their display of 'enthusiasm' and has the following to say about Quakers in his essay OF SUPERSTITION AND ENTHUSIASM:

On the other hand, it may be observed, that all enthusiasts have been free from the yoke of ecclesiastics, and have expressed great independence in their devotion, with a concept of forms, ceremonies, and traditions. The Quakers are the most egregious, though, at the same time, the most innocent enthusiasts that have been known: and are perhaps the only sect that have never admitted priests among them. The Independents, of all the English sectaries, approach nearest to the Quakers in fanaticism, and in their freedom from priestly bondage . . . In short, this observation is found in experience; and will also appear to be founded in reason, if we consider, that as enthusiasm arises from a presumptuous pride and confidence, it thinks itself sufficiently qualified to approach the Divinity, without any human mediation. Its rapturous devotions are so fervent, that it even images itself actually to approach him by way of contemplation and inward converse; which makes it neglect all those outward ceremonies and observances, to which the assistance of the priests appears so requisite in the eyes of their superstitious votaries. The fanatic consecrates himself, and bestows on his own person a sacred character, much superior to what forms and ceremonious institutions can confer on any other.

My second reflection with regard to these species of false religion is, that religions which partake of enthusiasm, are, on their first rise, more furious and violent than those which partake of superstition; but in a little time become more gentle and moderate . . . It is thus enthusiasm produces the most cruel disorders in human society; but in a little time becomes more gentle and moderate . . . but its fury is like that of thunder and tempest, which exhaust themselves in a little time, and leave the air more calm and serene than before. When the first fire of enthusiasm is spent, men naturally, in all fanatical sects, sink into the greatest remissness and coolness in sacred matters; there being no body of men among them endowed with sufficient authority, whose interest is concerned to support the religious spirit; no rites, no ceremonies, no holy observances, which may enter into the common train of life, and preserve the sacred principle from oblivion. Superstition, on the contrary, steals in gradually and insensibly; renders men tame and submissive; it is acceptable to the magistrate, and seems inoffensive to the people: till at last the priest, having established his authority, becomes the tyrant and disturber of human society, by his endless contentions, persecutions, and religious wars. How smoothly did the Roman church advance in her acquisition of power! But into what dismal convulsions did she throw all Europe, in order to maintain it! On the other hand, our sectaries, who were formerly such dangerous bigots, are now become free reasoners; and the Quakers seem to approach nearly the only regular body of Deists in the universe. the literati, or the disciples of Confucious in China.

Gilbert White *(1720-1793) was the vicar of Selborne in Hampshire. He was a devoted and greatly respected naturalist and his book,* THE NATURAL HISTORY OF SELBORNE, *is not only a classic of English literature but is also valuable for its keen and accurate observation of many of the aspects of life in the area in which he lived. The following is taken from a letter to Thomas Pennant:*

. . . In the spring and summer the women weed the corn; and enjoy a second harvest in September by hop picking. Formerly, in the dead months they availed themselves greatly by spinning wool, for making barragons, a genteel corded stuff, much in vogue at that time for summer wear; and chiefly manufactured at Alton, a neighbouring town, by some of the people called Quakers: but from circumstances this trade is at an end.★ The inhabitants enjoy a good share of health and longevity; and the parish swarms with children.

★ Since the above passage above was written, I am happy in being able to say that the spinning employment is a little revived, to the no small comfort of the industrious house-wife.

Quakers *in* THE GENTLEMAN'S MAGAZINE, *mid-18th century.*

There are references to Friends in various numbers of THE GENTLEMAN'S MAGAZINE, *the foremost monthly journal of the 18th century. The six items given here are the ones indexed that fall between 1747 and 1751.*

THE GENTLEMAN'S MAGAZINE *was founded in 1731 by Edward Cave, and first edited by him under the pseudonym of Sylvanus Urban, with considerable help in the 1740's from Samuel Johnson. In issues appearing in mid-century (vols xix and xx, 1749 and 1750), Johnson's tragedy* IRENE, *his periodical* THE RAMBLER *and his prologue written for a performance of* COMUS *benefitting Milton's needy granddaughter, are noted and quoted. It is satisfying to think of Johnson snorting over the references to Quakers in* THE GENTLEMAN'S MAGAZINE *at this period. These are of some interest in themselves. They also typify the span of the view in which Friends were held at this time as newsworthy by the world, a view which ranged, as these extracts do, from a touch of prurience and of merriment, through the factual reporting of matters of concern to Friends thought to be noteworthy (like London Yearly Meeting epistle), to a poetic tribute:*

April 1747: vol. xvii, p 170

A private LETTER sent from one QUAKER to another:

Friend John,

I desire thee to be so kind to go to one of those sinful men of the flesh, called an attorney, and let him take out an instrument with a seal fixed thereunto, by means whereof we may seize the outward tabernacle of George Green, and bring him before the lamb-skin men at Westminster, and teach him to do, as he would be done by: And so I rest thy friend in the light. R.G.

October 1747: vol. xvii, p 496

Dublin, Sept. 29. The people called Quakers waited on the lord lieu-tenant with an Address of Congratulation, which was spoken by John Barclay, and were graciously received.

December 1747: vol. xviii, p 571

Thursday 22nd. A man and a woman, quakers, walked through the streets at Bristol, Gloucester, Oxford, at separate times, clothed in hair sack-cloth, repeating something as they passed along, doing penance for a bastard child.

June 1749: vol. xix, p 269

Quaker's Letter.

Loving Friend Sylvanus Urban,

Looking the other day over some of thy valueable collections, I observed in vol. xvii, p 170, 'A private Letter sent from one Quaker to another,' signed R.G. As I do not believe it is thy design to make a scoff at any religious society of people, I am willing to inform thee, and the world, that that letter is not the form or manner of one of the people called Quakers writing to another, neither on that or any other subject. But if it came from one called a Quaker, the person was such a one who having★ turned the grace of our God into lasciv-iousness, writ it to ridicule the plain and christian-like manner and deportment of these people.

Thy information was also wrong in thy xviiith vol. page 571, where thou says, 'A man and a woman, quakers, walked through the streets . . .' [item above repeated in full]. For they are not in unity with the people called Quakers, nor were owned as such where they came.

– In publishing this thou will oblige,
Thy constant Reader and Friend, A.D.
Shropshire, 20th 4 mo. called June, 1749

February 1750: vol. xx, p 86

To a Virgin Speaker among the Quakers

To M.P. a Native of Ireland, now in England, visiting the Meetings of her Friends, the QUAKERS.

★ June 4th.

In thee, bright maid! accomplished, we behold
What antient seers of future times foretold.
Now poured on all the gifts of grace divine,
Our sons and daughters, undistinguished, shine.
The sacred energy the virgin feels,
And heavenly truths, with heavenly force reveals.
Warm'd from the skies with love of human kind.
Thy softer form conceals an hero's mind.
Each private tye dissolved, thy native shore,
Nor father's wishes, can retain thee more.
In vain old ocean swells the mountain-wave,
And loosed in vain, the madding tempests rave;
Thy fearless virtue ploughs th'Hibernian deeps,
Thy zeal, unwearied, constant vigil keeps:
Britannia's isle beholds, with wondering eyes,
Thy toils, that brave stern winter's frowning skies.
From town to town diffused the joyful sound,
Thy voice, persuasive, echoes wide around.
With joy attentive thousands hear thy tongue
Descant on good and evil, right and wrong;
From mystic phrases wholesome doctrines draw,
And moralize the rituals of the law.
From these, with evangelic skill displayed
The nobler plan that blest Emanuel laid;
'Tis thine to spread the gospel's brighter beam,
A Saviour's love is thy exhaustless theme!
A Saviour's death! a benefit to all!
Wide as the curse derived from Adam's fall.
His guilt removed, our own is all our share,
Our own, atoned by penitence and prayer.
Whate'er the Bigot's fierce religion be,
'Tis but a name, if 'tis not Charity.
The true criterion of our faith is deeds,
One act of love outweighs ten thousand creeds.

    While such the topics, thy discourses tend
To warm th' indifferent, and the stubborn bend;
To aid the weak, to startle the prophane,
To fix the wavering, mortify the vain;
Reduce the erring, the distressed to chear,
And almost make the Hypocrite sincere.

The peace, that conscious goodness gives, be thine;
Long may'st thou feel an influence all-divine;
Long by thy hearers be thy words revered,
Long may they practise what they heard.
Long scenes of bliss, on earth thy toils requite,
And endless raptures in the realms of light.

Oxfordsh. Jan. 10   PHILANTHROPOS

(We hear that the stature of this maiden is as remarkable as her accomplishments, being near 6 foot.)

October 1751: vol. xxi, p 475

HISTORICAL CHRONICLE, October 1751 . . . [London Yearly Meeting Epistle]

In a circular epistle from the yearly meeting at London to the quarterly meetings of the quakers in Great Britain, Ireland, and elsewhere, the account of sufferings this year (chiefly for tithes and church rates) amount in England and Wales to upwards of £3025, and in Ireland to upwards of £1760. There are four friends now remaining prisoners, two of them, in consequence of processes, in the ecclesiastical court.

Pursuant to the directions of the yearly Meeting for sufferings in London, and to the report of a committee, appointed by the said meeting to consider what advice might be necessary to give to friends, in relation to an Act made in the last session of Parliament for regulating the commencement of the Year, and correcting the Calendar now in use, this meeting hath thought convenient to communicate to the quarterly and monthly meetings of friends in Great Britain, Ireland, and America, the opinion of the said committee thereupon, which was,

> 'That in all the records and writings of friends, from and after the last day of the tenth month, called December next, the computation of time established by the said Act, should be observed; and that accordingly the first day of the eleventh month, commonly called January, next, shall be reckoned and deemed, by friends, the first day of the first month of the year 1752 . . .

> [Here follows a table showing the similar renumbering of all the following months.]

> And whereas for the more regular computation of Time, the same Act of Parliament doth direct, that "The natural Day next immediately following the second Day of September in the year 1752, shall be called reckoned and accounted to be the fourteenth Day of September, omitting for that time only the eleven intermediate Days of the common Calendar". The opinion of the said Committee, approved by the yearly Meeting, was, that friends should be sound

in the observance of this direction, and omit the said eleven nominal days accordingly.

The old-style calendar was still in force in 1749: hence 'A.D.' dates his letter 20th of the 4th month called June. The national transfer to the Gregorian calendar in 1752 is well enough understood in principle now. There is interest in seeing how it worked in detail, especially as sanctioned for Friends in the Yearly Meeting Epistle. Why Edward Cave should choose to give such full coverage to this in THE GENTLEMAN'S MAGAZINE *is intriguing. Perhaps he saw it as a good way of clarifying or reinforcing the change-over for his general readers. It is quite clear from this brief sample that, while Quakers were thought capable of providing amusement, at the same time their doings were accorded respect and given national newspaper coverage. A consistent study of references to Quakers throughout the history of* THE GENTLEMAN'S MAGAZINE *(it continued to 1914) might be instructive.*

LIFE OF JOHNSON – James Boswell (1709-1784)

31 July 1773: Next day, Sunday July 31, I [Boswell] told him I had been that morning at a meeting of the people called Quakers, where I had heard a woman preaching. JOHNSON. 'Sir, a woman's preaching is like a dog's walking on his hinder legs. It is not done well; but you are surprised to find it done at all.'

14 April 1775: Dr Johnson proceeded: 'Sir, there is a great cry about infidelity; but there are, in reality, very few infidels. I have heard a person, originally a Quaker, but now, I am afraid, a Deist,★ say, that he did not believe there were, in all England, above two hundred infidels'.

22nd March 1776: We next called on Mr Lloyd, one of the people called Quakers. He too was not at home, but Mrs Lloyd was, and received us courteously, and asked us to dinner. Johnson said to me, 'After the uncertainty of all human things at Hector's, this invitation came very well'. We walked about the town [Birmingham], and he was pleased to see it increasing . . .'

Mr Lloyd joined us in the street; and in a little while we met Friend Hector, as Mr Lloyd called him. It gave me pleasure to observe the joy which Johnson and he expressed on seeing each other again. Mr Lloyd and I left them together, while he obligingly shewed me some of the manufactures of this very curious assemblage of artificers. We all met at dinner at Mr Lloyd's, where we were entertained with great hospitality. Mr and Mrs Lloyd had been married the same year as their Majesties, and, like them, had been blessed with a numerous family of fine children, their numbers being exactly the same. Johnson said, 'Marriage is

★ This was Dr Brocklesby; cf Fox, Boswell Papers, x 216.

the best state for man in general, and every man is a worse man, in proportion as he is unfit for the married state'.

I have always loved the simplicity of manners, and the spiritual-mindedness of the Quakers, and talking with Mr Lloyd, I observed, that the essential part of religion was piety, a devout intercourse with the Divinity, and that many a man was a Quaker without knowing it . . .

As Dr Johnson had said to me in the morning, while we walked together, that he liked individuals among the Quakers, but not the sect; when we were at Mr Lloyd's, I kept clear of introducing any question concerning the peculiarities of their faith. But I having asked to look at Baskerville's edition of Barclay's APOLOGY, Johnson laid hold of it; and the chapter on baptism happening to open, Johnson remarked, 'He says there is neither precept nor practice for baptism, in the scriptures; that is false'. Here he was the aggressor, by no means in a gentle manner; and the good Quakers had the advantage of him; for he had read negligently, and had not observed that Barclay speaks of infant baptism, which they calmly made him to perceive.

15 May 1776: After dinner we had an accession of Mrs Knowles, the Quaker lady, well known for her various talents . . . Mr Wilkes held a candle to shew a fine print of a beautiful female figure which hung in the room, and pointed out the elegant contour of the bosom with the finger of an arch connoiseur. He afterwards, in a conversation with me, waggishly insisted, that all the time Johnson shewed visible signs of a fervent admiration of the corresponding charms of the Quaker.

. . . . . . 1777: Johnson observed that the differences among Christians are really of no consequence. Mrs Piozzi records (Anec. p 109):– 'In answer to the arguments urged by the Puritans, Quakers, etc. against showy decorations of the human figure, I once heard him [Johnson] exclaim:– 'Oh let us not be found, when our Master calls us, ripping the lace off our waistcoats, but the spirit of contention from our tongues! . . . Alas! Sir, a man who cannot get to heaven in a green coat will not find his way thither the sooner in a grey one.

[Footnote to vol. 3, p 188, 1887 Birbeck Hill edition]

15 April 1778: Boswell and Dr Johnson were entertained at the house of a Mrs Dilly. There he met a 'Quaker lady' called Mrs Knowles, whom Boswell described as 'ingenious'. Soames Jenyns had recently published his VIEW OF THE INTERNAL EVIDENCE OF THE CHRISTIAN RELIGION and in the discussion that took place Mrs Knowles held, against Jenyns, that friendship was a Christian virtue, enjoined by the Society. JOHNSON. 'Why, Madam, strictly speaking, he is right. All friendship is preferring the interest of a friend, to the neglect, or, perhaps, against the interest of others; so that an old Greek said, "He that has friends has no friend". Now Christianity recommends universal benevolence, to consider all men as our brethren, which is contrary to the virtue of friendship, as described by the ancient philosophers. Surely, Madam, your sect must approve of this, for you call all men friends.'. . .

Mrs Knowles mentioned, as a proselyte to Quakerism, Miss ----- [Jane Harry], a young lady well known to Dr Johnson, for whom he had shewn much affection; while she ever had, and still retained, a great respect for him. Mrs Knowles at the same time took an opportunity of letting him know 'that the amiable young creature was sorry at finding that he was offended at her leaving the Church of England and embracing a simpler faith;' and in the gentlest and most persuasive manner, solicited his kind indulgence for what was sincerely a matter of conscience. JOHNSON, (frowning very angrily), 'Madam, she is an odious wench. She could not have any proper conviction that it was her duty to change her religion, which is the most important of all subjects, and should be studied with all care, and with all the helps we can get. She knew no more of the Church which she left, and that which she embraced, than she did of the difference between the Copernican and Ptolemaick systems'.

28 April 1783: Having next day gone to Mr Burke's seat in the country, from whence I was recalled by an express, that a near relation of mine had killed his antagonist in a duel, and was himself dangerously wounded, I saw little of Dr Johnson till Monday, April 28, when I spent a considerable part of the day with him, and introduced the subject, which then occupied my mind. JOHNSON. 'I do not see, Sir, that fighting is absolutely forbidden in Scripture: I see revenge forbidden, but not self-defence.' BOSWELL. 'The Quakers say it is; "Unto him that smiteth thee on one cheek, offer also the other".' JOHNSON. 'But stay, Sir, the text is meant only to have the effect of moderating passion; it is plain that we are not to take it in a literal sense. We see this from the context, where there are other recommendations, which I warrant you the Quakers will not take literally; as, for instance, "From him that would borrow of thee, turn thou not away". Let a man whose credit is bad, come to a Quaker, and say "Well, Sir, lend me a hundred pounds;" he'll find him as unwilling as any other man. No, Sir, a man may shoot the man who invades his character, as he may shoot him who attempts to break into his house. So in 1745, my friend, Tom Cumming, the Quaker, said he would not fight, but he would drive an ammunition cart, and we know that the Quakers have sent flannel waistcoats to our soldiers, to enable them to fight better.'

> [Dr Franklin (Memoirs i, 177) says that when the assembly at Philadelphia, the majority of which were Quakers, was asked by New England to supply powder for some garrison, 'they would not grant money to buy powder, because that was an ingredient of war, but they voted an aid of £3000 to be appropriated for the purchase of bread, flour, wheat, or other grain'. The Governor interpreted other grain as gunpowder, without any objection ever being raised. Footnote to vol. IV, p 212, Birbeck Hill edition.]

TO THE SPADE OF A FRIEND – *William Wordsworth (1770-1850)*

Thomas Wilkinson, *the friend in question, was a Quaker farmer of Yanworth near Penrith and a close friend of William and Dorothy Wordsworth. The whole poem, although addressed to his spade, is an oblique tribute to him:*

Spade with which Wilkinson hath tilled
    his lands,
And shaped these pleasant walks by
    Emont's side,
Thou art a tool of honour in my hands;
I press thee, through the yielding soil,
    with pride.

Rare master has it been thy lot
    to know;
Long hast thou served a man to reason
    true;
Whose life combines the best of high
    and low,
The labouring many and the resting few;
Health, meekness, ardour, quietness
    secure,
And industry of body and of mind;
And elegant enjoyments, that are pure
As nature is:– too pure to be refined.

———

Who shall inherit Thee when death has laid
Low in the darksome cell thine own dear lord?
That man will have a trophy, humble
    Spade!
A trophy nobler than a conqueror's sword.

If he be one that feels, with skill to part
False praise from true, or, greater from
    the less,
Thee will he welcome to his hand and
    heart,
Thou monument of peaceful happiness.

He will not dread with Thee a toilsome
    day---
Thee his loved servant, his inspiring
    mate!

And, when Thou art past service, worn
    away,
No dull oblivious nook shall hide thy fate.
His thrift thy uselessness will never scorn;
An heir-loom in his cottage wilt Thou
    be:---
High will he hang thee up, well pleased
    to adorn
His rustic chimney with the last of Thee.

THE QUAKER – 'By a Lady' (1785)

This three-volume novel, published anonymously as 'By a Lady', is in the form of a series of letters, a type of novel popular amongst ladies of fashion and circulating libraries in the late 18th century. Fanny Burney's EVELINA is the epitome of the genre.

The main plot of the novel concerns two friends, young ladies of marriageable age; one, Selina Maynard, is a Quaker, the other, Octavia, is not. Selina is courted by Edward, who is not a Quaker and they become engaged to be married. They intend to postpone their actual marriage until Selina's widowed mother dies, leaving Selina in possession of the family fortune, bur there are complications. Selina's late father's will is found. By the terms of this, the family fortune is to be given to an unknown 'heir-at-law' if Selina survives her mother and contracts to 'marry out'. As this is just what she had bound herself to do, Selina feels she has no option but to write to the heir-at-law and renounce her inheritance; at the same time she ends her engagement to Edward, as she will not come to him penniless. She determines at first to abide strictly by the terms of her father's will. When the unknown heir-at-law at length arrives he proves to be someone to whom Edward had once rendered a great service; he also knows that he is a dying man to whom the inheritance is of no interest, so he turns it over to Edward. Edward persuades Selina to marry him, notwithstanding that she will be marrying out, but the assumption clearly is that she has fulfilled the terms of the will by her original renunciation of her fortune, so she is free to enjoy it now that it belongs legally to Edward, a somewhat devious argument.

There is no heart-searching in this novel over the principle of marriage within the Society and the severance which abandonment of it will cause, but it is clear that the authoress was acquainted with Quaker ways. There is a description of a visit by a non-Quaker to a Quaker household and a discussion over distinctive Quaker dress such as must have engaged many of the Quaker families of the day. In LETTER 1, Selina tells her friend that she had begun:

to perceive that true piety consists not in sober brown and plaited cambric . . . Why may not the prayers of a lovely woman, modernly adorned, be equally acceptable as those of a prim devotee, whose greatest sanctity consists in her apparel? May we not pray as fervently in lace as in cambric . . . (1; 13,15)

This argument must have been constantly heard in Quaker households with young and modish daughters, but Octavia suggests to her friend an argument calculated to appeal to vanity, not to the serious argument for the continuance of plain dress:

But let me intreat you will, in future, confine all your eulogiums to my small share of mental attractions, for, in personal ones, Selina Maynard far excels me; and, so far from her natural charms being in the least diminished by the sober garb she refers to as unbecoming, all the male sex have ever acknowledged that a pretty face is never so attractive as when enshrined in cambric and all the modest et-cetera of a quaker's habit. (1; 27)

Octavia goes to stay with Mrs Maynard and Selina. In a letter to her mother, LETTER IV, she writes at length about the sights of Nottingham and the district and then goes on to say something about the household. It is clear from the letter that Octavia feels it necessary to try to strengthen Selina's faith, which she sees as lacking a firm foundation and here perhaps the novel's authoress, in suggesting that Selina 'is at heart but half a quaker', is preparing the reader for the unbecoming ease with which Selina abandons her Quaker principles in favour of her worldy lover Edward. An extract from Octavia's letter to her mother runs as follows:

I have, as yet, said but little of our worthy friends . . . Nothing can more clearly stamp the worth of Mrs Maynard than the behaviour of her domestics; her whole household appears but a well-tuned instrument, every string of which unites to form a general harmony. Authority and tenderness are so sweetly blended in her deportment, even to the most menial of her servants, that obedience must necessarily become a pleasure . . .

Mrs Maynard, I find, was not of the same persuasion in her younger days, but became a proselyte; . . . but she pays as strict an observance to the forms of her religion as if she had from her earliest years been accustomed to the habit.

This [*earlier*] part of her life she mentions as seldom as possible before Selina, who, I am inclined to think, is at heart but half a quaker; and ever amiable as I am persuaded is her disposition, were an agreeable object to present himself, she would, I dare say, have few scruples . . . But as such an event would, I am sure, be productive of much uneasiness to Mrs Maynard, I ever endeavour to strengthen her attachment to the persuasion in which she has been educated . . .

In THE QUAKER, then, we have another of the fictions of the 18th century in which some of the conventions of Quaker behaviour are used to add interest and complications. Superficially these conventions may be presented as attractive, as honourable, even laudable; but when the plot demands it, Quaker integrity can be sacrificed without more ado. The will made by Selina's father is operative on her while she holds it valid; as soon as its effect is overturned Selina goes her own way with no thought of her father's intention and marries out. Such manipulation is of a piece with the treatment of Quaker heroines in plays like THE FAIR QUAKER OF DEAL and novels, a century later, like Marryat's JAPHET IN SEARCH OF A FATHER, and many other works of fiction. It is as if some authors felt the need to reassure society that Quakers were not, after all, incorruptible. In

*the treatment of the fortune and the response of the Quaker heroine to it there can be seen
traces of the 18th-century attitude to Quakers as concerned overmuch with money; they
would follow the road of worldly or romantic advantage with no thought of their faith and
are in the end just like the rest of the 'world's people'. But would such reassurance have
been necessary unless it was known that, in fact, the opposite was the case? The Quaker
portrayed by Defoe in MOLL FLANDERS is a genuinely good and kindly man; Charles
Lamb found no fault with Quaker principles and did not accuse Quakers of hypocrisy; his
criticism was that in their meetings they could fall victims to enthusiasm and fanaticism.
The world's view of Quakers was still an uneasy balance between admiration of the principles they held and total disbelief in the ability of any human being to guide his or her
life by them.*

ESSAY ON SLAVERY AND COMMERCE OF THE HUMAN SPECIES
— Thomas Clarkson (1760-1846) London 1786

*Early in his life Thomas Clarkson became a determined opponent of slavery and was
deeply involved in the anti-slavery movement of the late 18th and early 19th centuries.
His concern brought him into contact with Friends, who were closely connected with* William
Wilberforce *and the anti-slavery committee:*

The present age has also produced some zealous and able opposers of the *colo-
nial* slavery. For about the middle of the present century *John Woolman* and *Anthony
Benezet,* two respectable members of the religious society called Quakers, devoted
much of their time to the subject. The former travelled through most parts of
North America on foot, to hold conversations with the members of his own sect,
on the impiety of retaining those in a state of involuntary servitude, who had
never given them offence. The latter kept a free school at *Philadelphia* for the
education of the black people. He took every opportunity of pleading on their
behalf. He published several treatises against slavery, and gave an hearty proof of
his attachment to the cause, by leaving the whole of his fortune in support of that
school, to which he had so generously devoted his time and attention when alive.

Till this time it does not appear, that any bodies of men had collectively interested themselves in endeavouring to remedy the evil. But in the year 1754, the
religious society, called Quakers, publicly testified their sentiments upon the
subject, declaring, that, 'to live in ease and plenty by the toil of those, whom
fraud and violence had put into their power, was never consistent with
Christianity nor common justice'.

Impressed with these sentiments, many of this society immediately liberated
their slaves, and though such a measure appeared to be attended with considerable loss to the benevolent individuals, who unconditionally presented them with

their freedom, yet they adopted it with pleasure: nobly considering, that to possess a little, in an honourable way, was better than to possess much, through the medium of injustice. Their example was followed by the rest. A general emancipation of slaves in the possession of Quakers, at length took place; and so effectually did they serve the cause which they had undertaken, that they denied the claim of membership in their religious community, to all such as should hereafter oppose the suggestions of justice in this particular, either by retaining slaves in their possession, or by being in any manner concerned in the slave trade: and it is a fact, that through the vast tract of North America, there is not at this day a single slave in the possession of an acknowledged Quaker.

But though this measure appeared, as has been observed before, to be attended with considerable loss to the benevolent individuals who adopted it, yet, as virtue seldom fails of obtaining its reward, it became ultimately beneficial. Most of the slaves, who were thus unconditionally freed, returned without any solicitation to their former master, to serve them at stated wages, as free men. The work, which they now did , was found to be better done than before. It was found also, that a greater quantity was done in the same time. Hence less than the former number of labourers was sufficient. From these, and a variety of other circumstances, it appeared, that their plantations were considerably more profitable, when worked by free men, than when worked, as before, by slaves; and that they derived therefore, contrary to their expectations, a considerable advantage from their benevolence.

Animated by the example of the Quakers, the members of other sects began to deliberate about adopting the said measure . . . Should slavery be abolished there [*North America*], (and it is an event, which, from these circumstances, we may reasonably expect to be produced in time) let it be remembered, that the Quakers will have had the merit of its abolition.

Nor have their brethren here been less assiduous in the cause. As there are happily no slaves in this country, so they have not had the same opportunity of shewing their benevolence by a general emancipation. They have not, however, omitted to shew it as far as they have been able. At their religious meetings they have regularly inquired if any of their members are concerned in the iniquitous African trade. They have appointed a committee for obtaining every kind of information on the subject, with a view to its suppression, and, about three or four years ago, petitioned parliament on the occasion for their interference and support. I am sorry to add, that their benevolent application was ineffectual, and that the reformation of an evil, productive of consequences equally impolitick and immoral, are generally acknowledged to have long disgraced our national character, is yet left to the unsupported efforts of piety, morality and justice, against interest violence and oppression; and these, I blush to acknowledge, too strongly countenanced by the legislative assembly of a country, the basis of whose government is liberty.

Jeremy Bentham *(1748-1832) produced a number of works on ethics, jurisprudence, logic and political economy and it is by his political and ethical theory that he is principally remembered.* 'It is the greatest happiness of the greatest number which is the measure of right and wrong,' *a theory known as Utilitarianism.* THE INTRODUCTION TO PRINCIPLES OF MORALS AND LEGISLATION, *from which the following passage is taken, was published in 1789:*

The principle of asceticism, however, with whatever warmth it may have been embraced by its partisans as a rule of private conduct, seems not to have been carried to any considerable length, when applied to the business of government . . . Scarcely in any instance to any considerable length, by the religious: for the various societies of the Quakers, Dumblers, Moravians and other religionists, have been free societies, whose regimen no man has been astricted to without the intervention of his own consent. Whatever merit a man may have thought there would be in making himself miserable, no such notion seems ever to have occurred to any of them, that it may be a merit, much less a duty, to make others miserable . . .

Having explored how Quakers fared in prose and verse during the 18th century, let us see how the dramatists of the period dealt with them. It is interesting that Ezra Maxwell, *who has touched on this topic, concludes that 'the Quakers were more frequently characterised on stage than any other sect',* (PMLA XLV, 1) *and* Derek Forbes [2] *notes that at least 22 plays including Quakers were published before 1800, with more almost certainly to be discovered. In the early part of this period Quakers, as representing the extreme fringe of Puritanism, became the principal object of the reaction against it which followed the restoration of Charles II. They were ridiculed as figures of fun and the suggestion of lechery, which has been observed in some early doggerel, can also be seen in the portrayal of such figures as Obadiah Prim in* A BOLD STROKE FOR A WIFE, *by Susannah Centlivre, first shown in London in 1718.*

Plays representing this earlier view of Quakers are THE FAIR QUAKER OF DEAL, A BOLD STROKE FOR A WIFE *and* THE LOVER'S OPERA, *from which the following extracts are taken.*

THE FAIR QUAKER OF DEAL, *by Charles Shadwell, was first played in 1710, rewritten in 1773 and performed 180 times in London theatres alone until 1785, but in its treatment of Quakers it is in line with other early 18th century dramas. Dorcas Zeal, the fair Quaker, is betrothed to* Worthy, *a captain in the Navy, who is not of her religious persuasion, for which her sister* Arabella *scoffs at her:*

Arabella: (*to Worthy*). You see Worthy, I have done the work for you, reconciled even contradiction itself, made the flesh and the spirit unite, and joined an unsanctified brother of the wicked, to a sanctified sister of the godly ones.

Dorcas: Fie, sister, do not triumph in my weakness.

Arabella: Thy weakness! no, thy shame; with all thy boasted sanctity, to own before my face a carnal inclination.

When Dorcas announces her betrothal to her friend Belinda, *Belinda's comment is:* 'Why then the flesh has got the better of the spirit'. *As the plot unwinds, a local girl pretends to be Dorcas for a trick* – 'Well, if I do not act out the babe of grace, the former quaking saint, with as much outside sanctity as a new-entered nun, or an old mother abbess, I'll be content to truss up like James Nailer'. *At the end of Act Five there is a party and dancing and Dorcas is asked to dance by a character called* Rovewell; *she replies that the* 'females of our congregation, think it [*the*] vanity of vanities'. *The exchange continues as follows:*

Rovewell: Yes, in the country they may say so, but your London friends have all the gaiety imaginable; they sing, they dance, wear patches, and keep visiting days.

Dorcas: Well, rather than spoil your mirth, I will walk about.

Upon which Worthy says, 'I'll be pilot to my sweet Quaker,' *and Dorcas replies,* 'I desire no better friend for life'.

The assumption underlying the response of both Arabella and Belinda to the news of Dorcas' engagement is that 'spirit' and 'flesh' are sharply divided and that all Quakers should be all spirit alone. (How was it that Quakers ever married and had children?)

A BOLD STROKE FOR A WIFE, *by Susannah Centlivre, was first played in London in 1718, when it achieved considerable success. It continued to be presented on the London stage right up until the end of the 18th century and was equally popular in the provinces. The plot of the play is that* Obadiah Prim, *a Quaker, is one of the four guardians of the young heiress* Anne Lovely, *with each of whom she has to spend a quarter of the year. The permission of all four is necessary before she can marry. In the play, Anne's current quarter year is being spent with the Prims and there is much emphasis on her resentment of the imposition of Quaker 'peculiarities', including that of plain dress:*

Anne: Pray . . . are the pinched cap and formal hood the emblem of sanctity? does your virtue consist in your dress, Mrs Prim?

Mrs Prim: It doth not consist in cut hair, spotted face and a bare neck – Oh, the wickedness of the generation! The primitive women knew not the abomination of hooped petticoats . . .

Obadiah Prim is presented as sharing his wife's views, but this is a device on the part of the dramatist to emphasize the current view of Quakers as hypocrites and objects of ridicule. The following scene would have appealed to the comic sense of the audience:

Obadiah:	Not stripped of thy vanities yet, Anne? . . . Verily, thy naked bosom troubleth my outward man: I pray thee hide it Anne . . .
Anne:	Let me be quiet, I say. Must I be tormented thus for ever? . . . I cannot think my father meant this tyranny!
Obadiah:	Hark thee, dost thou call good counsel tyranny? Do I or my wife tyrannise, when we counsel thee in all love to put off thy tempting attire?
Anne:	Thou blinder of the world, don't provoke me – (*drawing Prim apart, aside:*) lest I betray your sanctity, and leave your wife to judge your purity. What were the emotions of your spirit – when you squeezed Mary by the hand last night in the pantry? . . . Ah! you had no aversion to naked bosoms, when you begged her to show you a little, little, little bit of her delicious bosom – don't you remember those words, Mr Prim?
Mrs Prim:	(*from a distance*) What does she say, Obadiah?
Obadiah:	She talketh unintelligibly, Sarah. (*Aside*) Which way did she hear this? . . . Verily, it troubleth me . . .

The remainder of the play is concerned with the efforts of Anne's suitor, Colonel Feignwell, *to gain her hand against the wishes of her guardians. When he achieves his end by a trick and in the dénouement discovers himself as an impostor who has deceived all four guardians by playing on their desire to keep Anne's fortune for themselves, Obadiah, who had no such sinister intention, accepts the situation and tells the other guardians he is glad their knavery has been discovered.*

The play, and the Quaker characters, were so popular that their names hit the national imagination, Obadiah Prim becoming an eponym for a (hypocritical) Quaker. This usage continued into the 19th century. And 'the real Simon Pure' is still with us as a phrase for the genuine article.

THE LOVER'S OPERA, *by William Rufus Chetwood, was first performed in 1729 and owed its initial success to the enthusiasm for ballad opera which followed the production of Gay's 'BEGGAR'S OPERA'. It ran for a 101 performances in the main London theatres up to 1754, but was not subsequently played. The Quaker in the opera is one Aminadab Prim (note the recurrence of the surname), who is old, rich and a suitor for the hand of one of the two daughters of Justice Dalton. Lucy, Dalton's pert maidservant, is horrified that her master should even entertain such an idea and responds to his plan as follows:* —

Lucy:	What, the Quaker?
Dalton:	He's rich.
Lucy:	Is he not too old?
Dalton:	He's rich, very rich.

A bowdlerised version of Quaker language is introduced for comic effect, as when Aminadab says: –

Verily, I do conceive thou utterest the word of truth. For as I did rest my head upon my bolster, in the night, in the darkness of the night, the Light said unto me——Aminadab arise, go thou to the damsel whom thou lovest, and she will turn unto thee; and thou shalt put unto her the truth, and her heart shall be towards thee; and Friends shall rejoice thereof.

One of the two songs in this ballad-opera, which include references to Quakers, is sung by Aminadab himself as a bent old man wooing a pretty young girl, the comic effect of which would have been highly appreciated by the audience:

> Wou'd that a gentle dove,
> Humh, on a Friend, look kind, ah!
> Who in purest love
> Humh! is to her inclin'd, ah!
>> Wou'd she bid the Quaker take her,
>> Mate for life to make her,
>>> Like turtle true
>>> He'd bill and coo – do
>> Take your upright Quaker.

But Justice Dalton's daughter is determined not to marry Aminadab and Lucy is bribed with a gift of £1,000 to take her place at the altar. When Aminadab discovers that he has been tricked he is curiously quite content with the outcome, as is Lucy also:

Aminadab:	I know no other remedy, on condition she will turn unto the Light – for she is not uncomely – she hath temptations – wilt thou listen to the word of Soberness?
Lucy:	I will truly.
Aminadab:	Then truly I will take the thousand pounds and thee.
Lucy:	I thank thee lovingly.

At this early period, although Friends were strongly advised not to marry out of the Society, nor to be married by a priest, they were not then disowned for doing so. The non-Quaker partner was urged to join Friends, as in her song at the end of the play Lucy is clearly very ready to do. With her ready tongue, she looks forward to the freedom given to Quaker women to preach, but Aminadab the Quaker has clearly been held up to ridicule, not only as an old man tricked into marrying a young girl substituted for the one of his choice, but by the casual allusions in his speeches to the temptations of the flesh and the importance of money. He takes the £1,000 before he takes the girl. Would he have accepted Lucy without it?

As the 18th century progressed good Christian moral values, as exemplified in the spread of Methodism, began to make their impact on the theatre and many playwrights were concerned to show in what was staged the triumph of good over evil. Performances of plays featuring Quaker characters became more rare, becoming perhaps only 1% of the whole, but this 1% showed Friends in a much more favourable light. The temper of the times had changed, manners were more polite, Quakers less aggressive and society perhaps showed a greater understanding of the principles and practices of the Society. This diminution of interest in Quakers by the late 18th-century dramatists may at first seem a paradox; at first glance one would perhaps expect that a greater knowledge of Quaker values would, in more enlightened times, have led to an increased rather than diminished presentation of Friends on the stage. Perhaps the answer is that by the end of the 18th century Quakerism was no longer something to be ridiculed, but had become an accepted part of the structure of society and no doubt respect was felt for such well-known and wealthy Friends as the Gurneys, Frys, Lloyds, Darbys and so on.

A two-act piece called THE QUAKER, *by* Charles Dibdin, *presented in 1775 exemplifies this change in attitude towards the end of the century. The piece was played 135 times in London before the century closed and the name part and lead is* Friend Steady, *a benevolent and mature Quaker, who is portrayed as a genuinely good man, sacrificing his own interest to that of the heroine of the play.*

But the most memorable presentation of Quakers on the stage was made by John O'Keeffe, *an Irish dramatist, in a play called* WILD OATS. *It was staged at Covent Garden theatre during the nine years before the close of the 18th century and continued to be part of London and provincial repertory until well into the 19th century. It was successfully revived by the Royal Shakespeare Company at the Aldwych Theatre in 1976. The plot of this play is extremely complex and, interestingly, O'Keeffe brings out the double aspect of Quakerism as he saw it. The heroine,* Lady Amaranth, *demonstrates what the dramatist saw as the virtues of Quakerism, in her open-minded generosity and kindness; her steward* Ephraim Smooth *the perhaps more conventional picture of self-righteous rectitude. Lady Amaranth does not use her title, allows her servants to call her simply 'Mary' and recognises virtue in any guise, so that she can say of a strolling player that he has* 'a gentle and generous heart'. *She is shown as capable of cheerfulness and has a genuine concern for the poor:*

Lady Amaranth:	. . . While I entertain the rich, the hearts of the poor shall also rejoice; I myself will now go forth into the adjacent hamlet, and invite all to hearty cheer.
Ephraim:	Yea, I will distribute among the poor, the good books thou didst desire me.
Lady Amaranth:	And meat and drink too, friend Ephraim. In the fullness of plenty they shall join in thanksgiving for those gifts which I abundantly possess.

Lady Amaranth befriends a company of strolling players and agrees to their putting on a performance of AS YOU LIKE IT *in her mansion. It is of course highly unlikely that a true Quaker in the later 18th century would have done this, but the difference between Lady Amaranth and her steward, the two opposing views of Quakerism, is beautifully brought out in the following piece of dialogue:*

Ephraim:	The mansion is now the tabernacle of Baal.
Lady Amaranth:	Then abide not in it.
Ephraim:	'Tis full of wicked ones.

Lady Amaranth:	Stay not amongst the wicked ones.
Ephraim:	Why dost thou suffer [*Rover, the leader of the players*] to put into the hands of thy servants books of tragedies, and books of comedies, prelude, interlude, yea, all lewd. My spirit doth wax wroth. I say unto thee, a play house is a school for the old dragon and a play book the prince of Beelzebub.
Lady Amaranth:	This is one, mark! (*reads*) 'Not the King's crown, nor the deputed sword, the marshal's truncheon, nor the judge's robe, become them with one half so good a grace as mercy doth. Oh, think on that, and mercy then will breathe within your lips like man new made'. Doth Beelzebub speak thus?

It has been generally considered that it was unthinkable then for Quakers to have any truck with the theatre, except for sending forth broadsides against it in the press and the epistles of London Yearly Meeting. But according to the minutes of Bristol Men's Meeting for 1699 one Martha Harford was arraigned to come before the Meeting for being '. . . at the late fair and the playhouse to the scandal and reproach of the religion . . . she hath professed', *and James Moore and Isaach Martindale were also* 'spoken to' *for being at a play. Quaker condemnation of the theatre does not seem to have been so whole-hearted among some Bristol Friends. Two generations later the banker industrialist Joseph Harford, together with two more Bristol Friends, Richard and William Champion, were amongst a group of shareholders putting up a new play-house in Bristol.*

At the close of the century young Betsy Gurney (later of course to become the prison reformer Elizabeth Fry), visiting London for the first time, attended theatres, dances routs and all the gaiety the city had to offer. Such behaviour was not common amongst strict Quakers, but the Gurneys of Norwich were far from being strict, although Betsy at that time was meditating on her experience of the ministry of the American Quaker William Savery. She did not, however, disapprove of the theatre; she simply found it dull and disappointing. What Janet Whitney has described as 'the hollow glitter of eighteenth-century drama'★ *failed to stir her imagination –* 'I had no other feeling when there than that of wishing it over . . . I still continue not to like plays. I think them so artificial that they are not to me interesting, and all seems so far from pure virtue and nature'. *Let this not entirely typical Quaker view stand as the reaction of some Quakers to their portrayal upon the 18th-century stage.*

★ *Janet Whitney:* Elizabeth Fry: Quaker Heroine, 1937, p 59

BATTERING RAMS

AGAINST

NEW ROME:

CONTAINING A

FARTHER DISCOVERY

OF

The Grand Hypocrisie

OF THE

LEADERS and TEACHERS

Of the PEOPLE Called

QUAKERS.

TOGETHER WITH

A Publick Challenge to meet *G. Fox*, *G. Whitehead*, *W. Penn*, and *S. Cater*, to prove Matters of Fact.

To which are Added

Some QUERIES propounded to their

PROTESTANT HEARERS,

Who are not of *G. F's* PARTY.

By *FRANCIS BUGG.*

I have laid a Snare for thee, and thou art taken, O BABYLON, and thou wast not aware: Thou art found, and also caught, because thou hast striven against the LORD. Put your selves in Array against BABYLON round about: All ye that bend the Bow, shoot at her, spare no Arrows. The LORD hath open'd his Armory, and hath brought forth the Weapons of his Indignation; for this is the Work of the LORD GOD of Hosts. Jer. 50. 14, 24, 25.

LICENSED, *Decemb.* 3. 1690.

LONDON, Printed for *Joh. Gwillim,* Book-seller, in *Bishops-gate-street,* over against the *Great James, Jan.* 12. 169⁰/₁.

Title page of Anti-Quaker Tract

Joshua Kaye (1773?-1851) of Leeds
From a silhouette with gilt-printed details, probably by Samuel Metford in 1852

Quaker Meeting (probably Gracechurch Street, London) by T. R. Rowlandson and A. C. Pepys: reproduction of a satirical aquatint engraving by Statdler: probably produced for Akermann's POETICAL MAGAZINE, 1809 as plate 64
[COURTESY OF FRIENDS HOUSE LIBRARY, LONDON: I52 & PIC L8/

John Porter Rodwell, Quaker Missionary, c.1910

[COURTESY OF JOANNA KIRKBY]

CHAPTER III

The Nineteenth Century

MANY READERS OF THIS ANTHOLOGY will already be aware of Charles Lamb's *affection for the Society of Friends. His lifetime (1775-1834) bridges the turn of the century; his approach to religion was formed by the Enlightenment, but his writings belong to the 19th century and it seems appropriate to place him here.*

There are two distinct strands in Lamb's approach to the Society. That probably better known to Quakers is revealed in his ESSAYS, *where he rises to heights of poetic appreciation for Quaker virtues of simplicity and quietness. But in his letters to his Quaker friend* Bernard Barton *the ambivalence of his approach appears both in his dislike of Quaker condemnation of the arts and in his rationalist rejection of enthusiasm and fanaticism.*

At one point in his early life he was strongly drawn towards Quakerism – 'Tell Lloyd [*Charles Lloyd*] I have had thoughts of turning Quaker' [1] – *thoughts inspired by his reading of William Penn's* NO CROSS, NO CROWN. *But he went on to attend a Quaker meeting, where he:*

saw a man under all the agitations and worship of a fanatic, who believed himself under the influence of some 'inevitable presence'. This cured me of Quakerism; I love it in the books of Penn and Woolman, but I detest the vanity of a man thinking he speaks by the Spirit, when what he says an ordinary man might say without all that quaking and trembling. [2]

and apart from his rejection of what he saw as fanaticism, he needed in his life pastimes deplored by the strict Quakers of London Yearly Meeting of the period: books, theatres, pictures, scandal and chit-chat – all the aesthetic and lighter sides of life so frowned on by the Society then. The Society spoke to him with two voices and the louder voice is heard in the following quotation from his essay on IMPERFECT SYMPATHIES:

I love Quaker ways and Quaker worship. I venerate the Quaker principles. It does me good for the rest of the day when I meet any of their people in my path. When I am ruffled or disturbed by an occurrence, the sight, or quiet voice of a Quaker acts upon me as a ventilator, lightening the air, and taking off a load from the bosom.

But he adds: 'I cannot like Quakers to live with them,' *and in the well-known essay on* A QUAKER MEETING *he commends the practice of silent worship in words which sit oddly beside his earlier experience:*

Reader, would'st thou know what true peace and quiet mean; would'st thou find a refuge from the noises and clamour of the multitude; would'st thou enjoy at once solitude and society; would'st thou possess the depth of thine own spirit in stillness, without being shut out from the consolatory faces of thy species; would'st thou be alone and yet accompanied; solitary, yet not desolate; singular, yet not without some to keep thee in countenance . . . Come with me into a Quakers' Meeting.

This essay is too long to be quoted in full, but there is one further paragraph which illustrates this aspect of Lamb's ambivalent approach to Quaker meetings:

More frequently a Meeting is broken up without a word having been spoken. But the mind has been fed. You go away with a sermon, not made with hands. You have been in the milder caverns of Trophonius; or as in some den, where that fiercest and savagest of all wild creatures, the TONGUE, that unruly member, has strangely lain tied up and captive. You have bathed with stillness – O When the spirit is sore fretted, even tired to sickness of the janglings and nonsense-noises of the world, what a balm and solace it is to go and seat yourself for a quiet half-hour upon some undisputed corner of a bench, among the gentle Quakers!

But for a rounded presentation of Lamb's view of the Society, the following extracts from letters to Bernard Barton in April 1823 and December 1828 must be considered. The first is on the subject of a poem sent by Bernard Barton to Lamb for his evaluation:

Your Society are eminent men of Business, and will probably regard you as an idle fellow, possibly disown you, that is to say, if you had put your name to a sonnet of that sort, but they cannot excommunicate. Mr Mitford, therefore, I thoroughly approve of printing the said verses. When I see any Quaker names to the Concert of Antient [*sic*] Music, or as Directors of the British Institution, or bequeathing medals to Oxford for the best classical themes, etc.——then I shall begin to hope they will emancipate you. But what as a Society can they do for you? you would not accept a Commission in the Army, nor they be likely to procure it; Posts in Church or State have they none in their giving; and if they disown you——think——you must live 'a man forbid'.[3]

There is a gentle, teasing humour in this first letter, but the second letter perhaps sums up Lamb's view of Quakers as he neared the close of his life. He continued to approve of Quaker principles even to the extent of believing that the church should move towards a more sympathetic view of them, but his rationalism continued to reject much Quaker practice:

I am for a Comprehension, as the Divines call it, but so that the Church shall go a good deal more than halfway over to the Silent Meeting house. I have ever said that the Quakers are the only Professors of Christianity as I read in the Evangiles; I say Professors – marry, as to practice, with their gaudy hot types and poetical vanities – they are much at one with the sinful.[4]

Saturday 19 June 1802: . . . Coleridge, when he was last here, told us that for many years, there being no Quaker meeting held at Keswick, a single old Quaker woman used to go regularly alone every Sunday, to attend the meeting-house alone, in that beautiful place among those fir trees, in that spacious vale, under the great mountain Skiddaw!!!

To a Beautiful Quaker – Lord Byron (1782-1824)

T. J. Wise *in his book A Bibliography of Byron puts the date of composition of these verses as 1806. They did not find a place in the edition of Byron's poem's of 1806, but were reprinted in 1810 in a short pamphlet, which gives the information that the lines were composed at the Crown Hotel, Harrogate in 1806:*

> Sweet Girl! Though only once we met,
> That meeting I shall ne'er forget;
> And though we ne'er may meet again,
> Remembrance will thy form retain.
> I would not say, 'I love,' but still
> My senses struggle with my will:
> In vain, to drive thee from my breast,
> My thoughts are more and more represt;
> In vain I check the raging sighs,
> Another to the last replies:
> Perhaps this is not love, but yet
> Our meeting I can ne'er forget.
> What though we never silence broke,
> Our eyes a sweeter language spoke;
> The tongue in flattering falsehoods deals,
> And tells the tale it never feels:
> Deceit the guilty lips impart,
> And hush the mandates of the heart;
> But soul's interpreters, the eyes,
> Spurn such restraint, and scorn disguise.
> And thus our glances oft conversed,
> And all our bosoms felt rehearsed,
> No spirit, from within, reproved us,
> Say rather,''twas the spirit moved us'.
> Though what they uttered, I repress,
> Yet I conceive thou'lt partly guess;

For as on thee my memory ponders,
Perchance to me thine also wanders,
This for myself, at least, I'll say,
Thy form appears through night, through day;
Awake, with it my fancy teems;
In sleep, it smiles in fleeting dreams;
The vision charms the hours away,
And bids me curse Aurora's ray
For breaking slumbers of delight
Which make me wish for endless night.
Since, Oh! whate'er my future fate,
Shall joy or woe my steps await,
Tempted by love, by storms beset,
Thine image I can ne'er forget.

Alas! again no more we meet,
No more our former looks repeat;
Then let me breathe this parting prayer,
The dictate of my bosom's care:
'May heaven so guard my lovely quaker,
That anguish never can o'ertake her;
That peace and virtue ne'er forsake her,
But bliss be aye her hearts partaker!
Oh! may the happy mortal, fated
To be, by dearest ties, related,
For her each hour new joys discover,
And lose the husband in the lover!
May that fair bosom never know
What 'tis to feel the restless woe
Which stings the soul, with vain regret,
Of him who never can forget'.

LETTERS FROM ENGLAND – *Robert Southey (1774-1843)*

Robert Southey published these LETTERS in 1807 as LETTERS OF ESPRITELLA, a fictitious Spanish traveller. The following extracts are taken form a long undated letter about Quakers and Quakerism. It should be remembered in reading them that this is an outsider's view of a Society still largely dominated by 18th-century Quietism. Similar criticisms of ministry to that made by Southey may be found in the extracts from Voltaire and Charles Lamb:

The most remarkable sect in this land of sectaries is unquestionably that of the Quakers. They wear a peculiar dress, which is in fashion such as grave people wore in the time of their founder, and always of some sober colour. They never uncover their heads in salutation, nor in their houses of worship; they have no form of worship, no order of priests, and they reject all the Sacraments. In their meeting-houses they assemble and sit in silence, unless any one should be disposed to speak, in which case they suppose him to be immediately moved by the Spirit; and any person is permitted to speak, women as well as men. These, however, are only a few of their peculiarities . . . What is truly extraordinary is, that though they seem to have advanced to the utmost limits of enthusiasm as well as of heresy, so far from being enthusiastic, they are proverbially deliberate and prudent: so far from being sullen and gloomy, as their prohibitions might induce you to suppose, they are remarkably cheerful: they are universally admitted to be the most respectable sect in England; and though they have a church without a priest-hood, and a government without a head, they are perhaps the best organized and most unanimous society that ever existed.

Were it not for their outrageous and insufferably heretical opinions, it might be thought that any government would gladly encourage so peaceable, so moral, and so industrious a people . . . One of the many remarkable circumstances belonging to this remarkable body is, that though they are now the least literate of all the English sects, they possess more ample collections of their own church history than any other Christian church, or even than any monastic order. If the acts of the Apostles had been as fully and faithfully recorded as the acts of the Quakers, what a world of controversy and confusion would have been prevented . .

Their preaching strikes a stranger as ludicrous. You may conceive what it must be, when the preacher imagines himself to be the organ of inspiration, and, instead of thinking what he shall say, watches for what he believes to be inter-nally dictated to him. Nothing in fact can be more incoherent than their discourse, and their manifest inferiority to those of any other sect ought to convince them of the fallacy of the opinion on which they proceed. That the admonition of the spirit, in other words the faculty of conscience, when it be wisely and earnestly cultivated is an infallible guide of conduct, may be and must be admitted, but that which will make a good man act well, will not always make him act wisely.

Their principles exclude them from all professions except that of physic, in which few can find employment: commerce therefore, may be considered as their sole pursuit; their plain and moderate habits lessen expense, and their indus-try insures success; they grow rich, and their children desert the society. The children of the rich find its restraints irksome, and are converted – not by strong arguments, not by incontrovertible authority, not by any honourable and worthy sense of duty, but by the pleasures of the card-table, the ball room, and the theatre. But the great agents in converting young Quakers to the established Church of England are the tailors. The whole works of Bellarmine could not produce such an effect upon them as a pattern-book of forbidden cloths and buttons. Nor could any reason be urged to them so forcibly as the propriety of appearing like other people, and conforming to the strict orthodoxy of fashion.

Odd as it may seem, this feeling has far more influence among the men than among the women of the society. The women who quit it usually desert for love, for which there is this good reason, that the Quakers have too much neglected the education of their sons. Women are easily converted in their youth; they make amends for this pliancy as they advance in life, and become the most useful diffusers of their own faith.

The diminution of the sect is not very manifest; and it is kept up by prose-lytes who silently drop in, for they no longer seek to make converts, and are even slow in admitting them. Perhaps these new members, if they are sufficiently numerous, may imperceptibly bring them nearer to the manners of the world in their appearance, and thus lessen the main cause of their decline.

THE ROUND TABLE: NORTHCOTE'S CONVERSATIONS: CHARACTERISTICS: – William Hazlitt, 1778-1830

THE ROUND TABLE was written during the years 1821-1822.

On the Tendency of Sects

There is a natural tendency in sects to narrow the mind.

The extreme stress laid upon differences of minor importance, to the neglect of more general truths and broader views of things, gives an inverted bias to the under-standing; and this bias is continually increased by the eagerness of controversy, and captious hostility to the prevailing system. A party-feeling of this kind once formed will insensibly communicate itself to other topics; and will be too apt to lead its votaries to contempt for the opinions of others, a jealousy of every difference of sentiment, and a disposition to arrogate all sound principle as well as understand-ing to themselves and those who think with them. We can readily conceive how such persons, from fixing too high a value on the practical pledge which they have given of the independence and sincerity of their opinions, come at last to entertain a suspicion of every one else as acting under the shackles of prejudice or the mask of hypocrisy. All those who have not given in their unqualified protest against doctrines and established authority, are supposed to labour under an acknowledged incapacity to form a rational determination on any subject whatever. Any argument, not having the presumption of singularity in its favour, is immediately set aside as nugatory. There is, however, no prejudice so strong as that which arises from a fancied exemption from all prejudice. For this last implies not only the practical conviction that it is right, but the theoretical assumption that it cannot be wrong. From considering all objections as in the manner 'null and void', the mind becomes so thoroughly satisfied with its own conclusions as to render any further examination of them superfluous, and confounds its exclusive pretensions to reason with the absolute possession of it . . . By the all-sufficiency of their merits in believing certain truths which have been 'hid from ages', they are elevated, in their own imagination, to a higher sphere of intellect, and are released from the necessity of pursuing the more ordinary tracks of inquiry. Their faculties are imprisoned in favourite dogmas, and they cannot break through the trammels of a sect. Hence we may remark a hardness and setness in the ideas of those who have been brought up in this way, an aversion to those finer and more delicate operations of the intellect, of taste, and genius, which require greater flexibility and variety of thought, and do not afford the same opportunity for dogmatical assertion and controversial cabal. The distaste of the Puritans, Quakers, &c. to pictures, music poetry, and the fine arts in general, may be traced to this source as much as to their affected disdain of them, as not sufficiently spiritual and remote from the gross impurity of sense . . . There is one quality common to all sectaries and that is, a principle of strong fidelity. They are the safest partisans and the steadiest friends. Indeed, they are almost the only people who have any idea of abstract attachment, either to a cause or to individuals, from a sense of duty, independently of prosperous or adverse circumstances, and in spite of opposition.

On the Quaker Objection to Colour

There is nothing to me more disagreeable than the abstract idea of a Quaker . . . They object to colours; and why do they object to colours? Do we not see that Nature delights in them? . . . Do we not find the most beautiful and dazzling colours bestowed on plants and flowers, on the plumage of birds, on fishes and shells, even to the bottom of the sea? All this profusion of ornament, we may be sure, is not in vain, To judge otherwise is to fly in the face of Nature, and substitute an exclusive and intolerant spirit in the place of philosophy, which includes the greatest variety of man's wants and tastes, and makes all the favourable allowances it can. The Quaker will not wear coloured clothes; though he would not have a coat to his back if men had never studied anything but the mortification of their appetites and desires. But he takes care of his personal convenience by wearing a piece of good broadcloth, and gratifies his vanity, not by finery, but by having it of a different cut from everybody else, so that he may seem better and wiser than they. Yet this humour, too, is not without its advantages; it serves to correct the contrary absurdity. I look upon the Quaker and the fop as two sentinels placed by nature at the two extremes of vanity and selfishness, and to guard, as it were, all the commonsense and virtue that lie between.

RURAL RIDES – William Cobbett (1763-1835)

Cobbett's RURAL RIDES were first published in his paper THE POLITICAL REGISTER and were later collected in book form. Cobbett had many hates: the 'Wen' as he called the city of London, all banks, stocks and shares, indeed anything to do with trading in money. Only farming was acceptable. His RURAL RIDES contain various references to Quakers, all of them rude; he regarded them as living on the backs of the workers, making money but doing nothing themselves:

26 July 1823: Thus the Quaker gets rich, and the poor devil of a farmer is squeezed into a gaol. The *Quakers* . . . are, as to the products of the earth, what the Jews are to gold and silver. How they profit, or, rather, the degree in which they profit, at the expense of those who own and those who till the land, may be guessed at if we look at their immense *worth*, and if we, at the same time, reflect that they never work. Here is a sect of *non-labourers*. One would think that their religion bound them under a curse *not to work*. Some part of the people of *all other* sects *work;* sweat at work; do something that is useful to other people; but here is a sect of buyers and sellers. They *make* nothing; they *cause nothng to come*; they breed as well as other sects; but they make none of the raiment or houses, and cause none of the food to come. In order to justify some measure for paring the nails of this grasping sect, it is enough to say of them, which we may with perfect truth, that, if all the other sects were to act like them, *the community must perish*. This is quite enough to say of this sect, of the monstrous privileges of whom we shall, I hope, one of these days, see an end. If I had the dealing with them, I would soon teach them to use the *spade* and the *plough*, and the *musket* too when necessary.

7 August 1823: I got to Thurley about sunset, without experiencing any inconvenience from the wet. I have mentioned the state of the corn as far as Selborne. On this side of that village I find it much forwarder than I found it between Selborne and Ropley Dean. I am here got into some of the very best barley-land in the kingdom; a fine, buttery, stoneless loam, upon a bottom of sand or sandstone. Finer barley and turnip-land it is impossible to see. All the corn is good here. The wheat not a heavy crop; but not a light one; and the barley all the way along from Headley to this place as fine, if not finer, that I ever saw it in my life. Indeed I have not seen a bad field of barley since I left the Wen. The corn is not so forward here as under Portsdown Hill; but some farmers intend to begin

65

reaping wheat in a few days. It is monstrous to suppose that the price of corn will not come down. It must come down, good weather or bad weather. If the weather be bad, it will be so much the worse for the farmer, as well as for the nation at large, and can be of no benefit to any human being but the Quakers, who must now be pretty busy, measuring the crops all over the kingdom. It will be recollected that, in the Report of the Agricultural Committee of 1821, it appeared from the evidence of one HODGSON, a partner of CROPPER, BENSON, and Co., Quakers, of Liverpool, that these Quakers sent a set of corn-gaugers into several counties, just before every harvest; that these fellows stopped here and there, went into the fields, measured off square yards of wheat, clipped off the ears, and carried them off. These they afterwards packed up and sent to Cropper and Co at Liverpool. Then the whole of the packets were got together, they were rubbed out, measured, weighed, and an estimate made of the amount of the coming crop. This, according to the confession of Hodgson himself, enabled these Quakers to speculate in corn, with the greater chance of gain. This has been done by these men for many years. Their disregard of worldly things; their desire to lay up treasures in heaven; their implicit yielding to the Spirit; these have induced them to send their corn-gaugers over the country regularly year after year; and I will engage that they are at it this moment. The farmers will bear in mind, that the New Trespass-law, though clearly not intended for any such purpose, enables them to go and seize by the throat any of these gaugers that they may catch in their fields. They could not do this formerly; to cut off standing corn was merely a trespass, for which satisfaction was to be attained by action at law. But now you can seize the caitiff who is come as a spy amongst your corn. Before, he could be off and leave you to find out his name as you could; but now, you can lay hold of him, as Mr Deller did of the Duke's man, and bring him before a Magistrate at once. I do hope that the farmers will look sharp out for these fellows, who are neither more nor less than so many spies. They hold a great deal of corn; they want a blight, mildew, rain, hurricanes; but happy I am to see that they will get no blight, at any rate. The grain is formed; everywhere every body tells me that there is no blight in any sort of corn, except beans.

3 Sept 1826, Devizes: Before I speak of my ride from Warminster to this place, I must once more observe, that Warminster is a very nice town; every thing belonging to it is *solid* and *good* . . . It is a great *cornmarket*: one of the greatest in this part of England; and here things are still conducted in the good, old honest fashion. The corn is brought and pitched in the market *before* it is sold; and, when sold, it is *paid for on the nail*; and all is over and the farmers and millers gone home by daylight. Almost everywhere else the corn is sold by *sample*; it is sold by *juggling* in a corner; the parties must meet and drink first; it is night work; there is no *fair and open market*; the mass of the people do not know *what the prices are*; and all this favours that monopoly which makes the corn change hands many times, perhaps, before it reaches the mouth, leaving a profit in each of hands, and which monopoly is, for the greater part, carried on by the villanous tribe of *Quakers*, *none of whom ever work*, and all of whom prey upon the rest of the community, as those infernal devils, the wasps, prey upon the bees . . . the farmer, who produces corn and meat and wool and wood, is not taxed; nor is the coach-master who buys the corn and gives it to his horses, nor the miller who buys it to change the state of it, nor the baker who buys the flour to change its state; nor is the manufacturer who buys the wool to change its state; and so on: but the Jew, or Quaker, the *mere dealer*, who buys the corn of the producer to sell it to the miller, and to deduct a *profit*, which must, at last *fall upon the consumer*: this Jew, or Quaker, or self-styled Christian, who acts the part of Jew or Quaker, is *taxed by the King of Spain*; and for this, I applaud the King of Spain. If we had a law like this, the pestiferous sect of non-labouring, sleek and fat hypocrites could not exist in England. But, ours is, altogether, a *system of monopolies*, created by taxation and paper-money, from which monopolies are inseparable. It is noto-rious, that the brewer's monopoly is the master even of the Government; it is well known to all who examine and reflect, that a very large part of our bread comes to our mouths loaded with the profits of nine or ten, or more, different dealers; and, I shall, as soon as I have leisure, PROVE as clearly as any thing ever was proved, that the people pay *two millions of pounds* a year in consequence of the MONOPOLY IN TEA! that is to say, they pay two million a year *more than they would pay* were it not for the monopoly; and, mind, I do not mean the monopoly of the *East India Company*: but, the *monopoly of the Quaker and other Tea Dealers*, who buy the tea of that Company! The people of this country are eaten up by monopolies. These compel those who labour to maintain those who do not labour; and hence the success of the crafty crew of Quakers, the very existence of which sect is a disgrace to the country.

REDGAUNTLET – *Sir Walter Scott (1771-1832)*

REDGAUNTLET was first published in 1824. The Quaker makes his appearance thus:

I observed that the rider who approached us slackened his horse's pace from a slow trot to a walk, as if desirous to suffer us to proceed, or at least to avoid pass-ing us at a spot where the difficulty of doing so must have brought us very close to each other. You know my old failing, Alan, and that I am always willing to attend to any thing in preference to the individual who has for the time posses-sion of the conversation.

Agreeably to this amiable propensity, I was internally speculating concern-ing the cause of the rider keeping aloof from us, when my companion, elevat-ing his deep voice so suddenly and so sternly, as at once to recall my wandering thoughts, exclaimed, 'In the name of the devil, young man, do you think that others have no better use for their time than you have, that you oblige me to

67

repeat the same thing to you three times over? – Do you see, I say, yonder thing at a mile's distance that looks like a finger-post, or rather like a gallows? – I would it had a dreaming fool hanging upon it, as an example to all meditative moon-calves! – Yon gibbet-looking pole will guide you to the bridge, where you must pass the large brook; then proceed straight forwards, till several roads divide at a cairn. – Plague on thee, thou art wandering again'!

It is indeed quite true that at this moment the horseman approached us, and my attention was again called to him as I made way to let him pass. His whole exterior at once showed that he belonged to the Society of Friends, or as the world and the world's law call them, Quakers. A strong and useful iron-grey galloway showed, by its sleek and good condition, that the merciful man was merciful to his beast. His accoutrements were in the usual unostentatious, but clean and serviceable order, which characterizes these sectaries. His long surtout of dark-grey superfine cloth descended to the middle of his leg, and was buttoned up to his chin, to defend him against the morning air. As usual, his ample beaver hung down without button or loop, and shaded a comely and placid counte-nance, the gravity of which appeared to contain some seasoning of humour, and had nothing in common with the pinched puritanical air affected by devotees in general. The brow was open and free from wrinkles, whether of age or hypocrisy. The eye was clear, calm, and considerate, yet appeared to be disturbed by appre-hension, not to say fear, as, pronouncing the usual salutation of, 'I wish thee a good morrow, friend,' he indicated, by turning his palfrey close to one side of the path, a wish to glide past us with as little trouble as possible – just as a trav-eller would choose to pass a mastiff of whose peaceable intentions he is by no means confident.

But my friend, not meaning, perhaps, that he should get off so easily, put his horse quite across the path, so that, without plunging into the slough, or scram-bling up the bank, the Quaker could not have passed him. Neither of these was an experiment without hazard greater than the passenger seemed willing to incur. He halted, therefore, as if waiting till my companion should make way for him; and as they sat fronting each other, I could not help thinking that they might have formed no bad emblem of Peace and War; for although my conductor was unarmed, yet the whole of his manner, his stern look, and his upright seat on horseback, were entirely those of a soldier in undress. He accosted the Quaker in these words – 'So ho! friend Joshua – thou art early to the road this morning. Has the spirit moved thee and thy righteous brethren to act with some honesty, and pull down yonder tide-nets that keep the fish from coming up the river?'

'Surely, friend, not so,' answered Joshua firmly, but good humouredly at the same time; 'thou canst not expect that our own hands should pull down what our own purses established. Thou killest the fish with spear, line, and coble-net; and we, with snares and with nets, which work by the ebb and the flow of the tide. Each doth what seems best in his eyes to secure a share of the blessing which Providence hath bestowed on the river, and that within his own bounds. I prithee, seek no quarrel against us, for thou shalt have no wrong at our hand.'

'Be assured I will take none at the hand of any man, whether his hat be cocked or broad-brimmed,' answered the fisherman. 'I tell you in fair terms, Joshua Geddes, that you and your partners are using unlawful craft to destroy the fish in the Solway by stake-nets and wears; and that we, who fish fairly, and like men, as our fathers did, have daily and yearly less sport and less profit. Do not think gravity or hypocrisy can carry it off as you have done. The world knows you, and we know you. You will destroy the salmon which make the livelihood of fifty poor families, and then wipe your mouth, and go to make a speech at Meeting. But do not hope it will last thus. I give you fair warning, we will be upon you one morning soon, when we will not leave a stake standing in the pools of the Solway; and down the tide they shall every one go, and well if we do not send a lessee along with them.'

'Friend,' replied Joshua, with a constrained smile, 'but that I know thou dost not mean as thou say'st, I would tell thee that we are under the protection of this country's laws; nor do we the less trust to obtain their protection, that our principles permit us not, by any act of violent resistance, to protect ourselves.'

'All villainous cant and cowardice,' exclaimed the fisherman,'and assumed merely as a cloak to your hypocritical avarice.'

'Nay, say not cowardice, my friend,' answered the Quaker, 'since thou knowest there may be as much courage in enduring as in acting; and I will be judged by this youth, or by any one else, whether there is not more cowardice – even in the opinion of that world whose thoughts are the breath in thy nostrils – in the armed oppressor, who doth injury, than in the defenceless and patient sufferer, who endureth it with constancy.'

'I will change no more words with you on the subject,' said the fisherman, who, as if something moved at the last argument which Mr Geddes had used, now made room for him to pass forward on his journey. – 'Do not forget, however,' he added, 'that you have had fair warning, nor suppose that we will accept of fair words in apology for foul play. These nets of yours are unlawful——they spoil our fishings——and we will have them down at all risks and hazards. I am a man of my word, friend Joshua'.

'I trust thou art,' said the Quaker; 'but thou art the rather bound to be cautious in rashly affirming what thou wilt never execute. For I tell thee, friend, that though there is as great a difference between thee and one of our people, as there is between a lion and a sheep, yet I know and believe thou has so much of the lion in thee, that thou wouldst scarce employ thy strength and thy range upon that which professeth no means of resistance. Report says so much good of thee, at least, if it says little more.'. . .

The Quaker and I proceeded on our journey for some time in silence; he restraining his soberminded steed to a pace which might have suited a much less active walker than myself, and looking on me from time to time with an expression of curiosity mingled with benignity. For my part, I cared not to speak first. It happened I had never before been in company with one of this particular sect, and, afraid that in addressing him I might unwittingly infringe upon some of their prejudices or peculiarities, I patiently remained silent. At length he asked me, whether a I had been long in the service of the Laird, as men called him.

I repeated the words 'in his service?' with such an accent of surprise as induced him to say, 'Nay, but, friend, I mean no offence; perhaps I should have said in his society – an intimate, I mean, in his house?'

'I am totally unknown to the person from whom we have just parted,' said I, 'and our connexion is only temporary – He had the charity to give me his guidance from the Sands, and a night's harbourage from the tempest. So our acquaintance began, and there is likely to end; for you may observe that our friend is by no means apt to encourage familiarity.'

'So little so,' answered my companion, 'that thy case is, I think, the first in which I ever heard of his receiving any one into his house; that is, if thou hast really spent the night there.'

'Why should you doubt it?' replied I; 'there is no motive I can have to deceive you, nor is the object worth it.'

'Be not angry with me,' said the Quaker; 'but thou knowest that thine own people do not, as we humbly endeavour to do, confine themselves within the simplicity of truth, but employ the language of falsehood, not only for profit, but for compliment, and sometimes for mere diversion. I have heard various stories of my neighbour; of most of which I only believe a small part, and even then they are difficult to reconcile with each other. But this being the first time I ever heard of his receiving a stranger in his dwelling, made me express some doubts. I pray thee let them not offend thee.'

'He does not,' said I, 'appear to possess in much abundance the means of exercising hospitality, and so may be excused from offering it in ordinary cases.'

'That is to say, friend,' replied Joshua, 'thou has supped ill, and perhaps break-fasted worse. Now my small tenement, called Mount Sharon, is nearer to us by two miles than thine inn; and although going thither may prolong thy walk, as taking thee of the straighter road to Shepherd's Bush, yet methinks exercise will suit thy youthful limbs, as well as a good plain meal thy youthful appetite. What say'st thou, my young acquaintance?'

'If it puts you not to inconvenience,' I replied; for the invitation was cordially given, and my bread and milk had been hastily swallowed, and in small quantity.

'Nay,' said Joshua, 'use not the language of compliment with those who renounce it. Had this poor courtesy been very inconvenient, perhaps I had not offered it.'

'I accept the invitation then,' said I, 'in the same good spirit in which you give it.'

The Quaker smiled, reached me his hand, I shook it, and we travelled on in great cordiality with each other. The fact is, I was much entertained by contrast-ing in my own mind, the open manner of the kind-hearted Joshua Geddes, with the abrupt, dark, and lofty demeanour of my entertainer on the preceding evening. Both were blunt and unceremonious; but the plainness of the Quaker had the character of devotional simplicity, and was mingled with the more real kindness, as if honest Joshua was desirous of atoning, by his sincerity, for the lack of external courtesy.

MEMOIR OF THOMAS BEWICK, written by himself.

Thomas Bewick (1753-1828) *was born in Northumberland, the son of a small farmer. He became a famous wood-engraver and is particularly well known for his HISTORY OF BRITISH BIRDS, published in two separate volumes in 1797 and 1804. His MEMOIR was not published by his daughter Jane until 1862, but it seems appropriate to place it at about the year of his death:*

There is another sect growing into great importance as a religious society, and that is the Quakers——the 'Friends' as they properly denominate themselves. They have many excellent rules laid down by which to regulate their conduct in life, and with all their peculiarities, their simplicity of manners commands the respect of the thinking part of mankind. They have, it is true, been characterised as 'English Jews' by some, and others have said of them that they are not now a religious sect like the Methodists——'they are an aristocratic civil community', a trading company, and a set of respectable, industrious, economical, money-getting disciplinarians, who profess no more practical religion than the members of the church of England. This may no doubt be the opinion of some, but I could never form such a one of, at least, the great majority of them, for they appear to me to deserve a better character. I wish, indeed, to see them leave off a part of their Puritanical appearance, and some other stiffnesses in their deport-ment. Were all men Quakers, I think the world would have a very sombre appear-ance, but this is balanced by their keeping their word, by their detestation of war, and by their constant endeavours to live in peace with all men. I have often wondered at their rejecting music. Music is an emanation from heaven; it is perfectly natural to man to drive away gloom and to solace and to cheer him . . . (pp 101-102)

THE GREVILLE MEMOIRS – Charles Cavendish Fulke Greville (1794-1865)

Charles Greville *was a politician who from 1820 to 1860 kept a detailed record of the political life of his time. Here he describes the Quakers presenting a* Loyal Address *to King William IV on his accession to the throne. Quakers of course, traditionally refused to use the title 'Majesty':*

Previously the King received the address of the departing Ministers, and then that of the Quakers, presented by William Allen; they were very prim and respectable persons; their hats were taken off by each other in the room before the Throne Room, and they did not bow, though they seemed half-inclined: they made a very loyal address, but without "Majesty" and said "O King". There was a question after his answer what they should do. I thought it was whether they should kiss hands, for the king said something to Peel, who went and asked them, and I heard the King say, "Oh, just as they like; they needn't if they don't like; it's all one".

PAST AND PRESENT – Thomas Carlyle (1795-1881)

Ralph Waldo Emerson, *in his introduction to* PAST AND PRESENT, *which was first published in 1843, called it the* Iliad *of English woes. Carlyle, deeply disturbed by the* 'calamity of the times' *(Emerson) which he sees in the viciousness and lack of honesty in many aspects of industrial life, sets out by comparing the practices of distant ages with the present. He seeks to show how the situation may be remedied and finds much of value in the industrial mores of the good Quaker. It is interesting to note that by 1843 music was no longer forbidden to Quakers:*

In a Printed Sheet of the assiduous, much abused, and truly useful Mr Chadwick's containing queries and responses from far and near as to this great question, 'What is the effect of education on working-men, in respect of their value as mere workers?' the present Editor, reading with satisfaction a decisive unanimous verdict as to Education, reads with inexpressible interest this special remark, put in by way of marginal incidental note, from a practical manufacturing Quaker, whom, as he is anonymous, we will call Friend Prudence. Prudence keeps a thousand workmen; has striven in all ways to attach them to him, has provided conversational soirées; play grounds, bands of music for the young ones; went even 'the length of buying them a drum', all of which has turned out to be an excellent investment. For a certain person, marked here by a black stroke, whom we name Blank, living over the way, – he also keeps somewhere above a thousand men, but has done none of these things for them, nor any other thing, except due payment of the wages by supply-and-demand. Blank's workers are perpetually getting into mutiny, into broils and coils; every six months, we suppose, Blank has a strike; every one month, every day and every hour, they are fretting and obstructing the shortsighted Blank; pilfering from him, wasting and idling for him, omitting and committing for him. 'I would not' says Friend Prudence, 'exchange my workers for his with seven thousand pounds to boot'.

Right, O honourable Prudence; thou art wholly in the right: Seven thousand pounds even as a matter of profit for this world, nay for the mere cash-market of this world! And as a matter of profit not for this world only, but for the other world and all worlds, it outweighs the Bank of England!——Can the sagacious reader descry here, as it were the outmost inconsiderable rock-ledge of a universal rock-foundation, deep once more as the Centre of the World, emerging so, in the experience of this good Quaker, through the Stygian mud-vortexes and general Mother of Dead Dogs, whereon, for the present, all swags and insecurity hovers, as if ready to be swallowed? . . . (pp 268-269)

I revert to Friend Prudence the good Quaker's refusal of 'seven thousand pounds to boot'. Friend Prudence's practical conclusion will, by degrees, become that of all rational and practical men whatsoever. On the present scheme and principle, Work cannot continue. Trades' Strikes, Trades' Unions, Chartism; mutiny, squalor, rage and desperate revolt, growing ever more desperate, will go on their way. As dark misery settles down on us, and our refuges of lies fall in pieces one after one, the hearts of men, now at last serious, will turn to refuges of truth. The eternal stars shine out again, as soon as it is dark enough.

Thomas Carlyle published his LIFE OF JOHN STERLING *in 1851. The following is an extract from part III, chapter II, referring to early 1840:*

At Falmouth Sterling had been warmly welcomed by the well-known Quaker family of the Foxes, principal people in that place, persons of cultivated opulent habits, and joining to the fine purities and pieties of their sect a reverence for human intelligence in all kinds; to whom such a visitor as Sterling was naturally a welcome windfall. The family had grave elders, bright cheery younger branches, men and women; truly amiable all, after their sort: they made a pleasant image of home for Sterling in his winter exile. 'Most worthy, respectable and highly cultivated people, with a great deal of money among them' writes Sterling in the end of February; 'who make the place pleasant to me. They are connected with all the large Quaker circle, the Gurneys, Frys, &c., and also with Buxton the Abolitionist. It is droll to hear them talking of all the common topics of science, literature and life, and in the midst of it: "Does thou know Wordsworth?" or, "Did thou see the Coronation?" or, "Will thou take some refreshment?" They are very kind and pleasant people to know.'

THE NOCTES AMBROSIANAE *are a series of dialogues which appeared in* BLACKWOOD'S MAGAZINE *in the early 19th century. They are by various hands, but the principal author was* John Wilson, *who fictionalised himself in the 'Noctes' as* Christopher North. *The following is an extract from dialogue which appeared in* BLACKWOOD'S *for April 1831. The characters are* Christopher North *and the Ettrick Shepherd, a representation of another real person,* James Hogg, *the poet:*

North: Your head, my dear James, is now touching Howitt's Book of the Seasons. Prig and pocket it. 'Tis a Jewel.

[The SHEPHERD seizes it from the shelf and acts as per order.]

Shepherd: Is Nottingham far intil England, sir? For I would really like to pay the Hooitts a visit this simmer. Thae Quakers are, what ane micht scarcely opine frae first principles, a maist poetical Christian seck. There was Scott o' Amwell, wha wrote some simplish things in a preservin speerit o' earnestness; – there is Wilkinson, yonner, wha wons on a beautifu' banked river, no far aff Peerith (is't the Eamont, think ye?) the owther o' no a few pomes delichtfu' in their domesticity – auld bachelor though he be – nae warld-sick hermit, but an enlightened labourer o' love, baith in the kitchen and flower garden o' natur; – lang by letter has me and Bernard Barton been acquent, and verily he is ane o' the mildest and modestest o' the Muses' sons, nor wanting a thochtfu' genie, that aften gies birth to verses that treasure themselves in folk's hearts; – the best scholar amang a' the Quakers is Friend Wiffen, a capital translator, Sir Walter tells me, o' poets wi' foreign tongues, sic as Tawso, and wi' an original vein too, sir, which has produced, as I opine, some verra pure ore; – and feenally, the Hooitts, the three Hooitts, – na, there may be mair o' them for aught I ken, but I'se answer for William and Mary, husband and wife, and oh! but they're weel met; and eke for Richard, (can he be their brither?) and wha's this was telling me about anither brither o' Wullie's, a Dr Godfrey Hooitt, ane o' the best botanists in a' England, and a desperate beetle-hunter?

North: Entomologist, James. A man of science.

Shepherd: The twa married Hooitts I love just excessively, sir. What they write canna fail o' bein' poetry, even the maist middlin o't, for it's aye wi' them the ebullition o' their ain feeling, and their ain fancy, and whenever that's the case, a bonny word or twa will drap itself intil ilka stanzy, and a sweet stanzy or twa intil ilka pome, and sae they touch and sae they sune win a body's heart; and frae readin their byuckies ane wushes to ken theirsels, and indeed do ken theirsels, for their personal characters are revealed in their volumms, and methinks I see Wully and Mary –

North: Strolling quietly at eve or morn by the silver Trent –

Shepherd: No sae silver, sir, surely, as the Tweed?

North:	One of the sincerest streams in all England, James.
Shepherd:	Sincere as an English sowl that caresna wha looks intil't, and flows bauldly alang whether reflectin clude or sunshine.
North:	Richard, too, has a true poetical feeling, and no small poetical power. His unpretending volume of verses well deserves a place in the library along with those of his enlightened relatives – for he loves nature truly as they do, and nature has returned his affection.
Shepherd:	But what's this Byuck o' the Seasons?
North:	In it the Howitts have wished to present us with all their poetic and picturesque features – a Calendar of Nature, comprehensive and complete in itself – which, on being taken up by the lover of nature at the opening of each month, should lay before him in prospect all the objects and appearances which the month would present, in the garden, in the field, and the waters – yet confining itself solely to those objects. Such, in their own words, is said to be their aim.
Shepherd:	And nae insignificant aim either, sir. Hae they hit it?
North:	They have. The scenery they describe is the scenery they have seen.
Shepherd:	That circling Nottingham.
North:	Just so, James. Their pictures are all English.
Shepherd:	They show their sense in stickin to their native land – for unless the heart has brooded, and the eeen brooded too, on a' the aspecks o' the outer warld till the edge o' ilka familiar leaf recalls the name o' the flower, shrub or tree frae which it has been blawn by the wund, or drapped in the caum, the poet's haun 'ill waver, and his picture be but a haze. In a' our warks, baith great an' sma', let us be national; an' thus the true speerit o' ae kintra 'ill be breathed intil anither, an' pervaded wi' poetry and love.
North:	As a proof, James, of their devotedness to merry England –
Shepherd:	No a whit less merry that it contains a gude mony Quakers.
North:	——our Friends have described the year, without once alluding——as far as I have observed——to the existence of Thomson.
Shepherd:	Na——that is queer an' comical eneugh;——nor can I just a'thegither appruve o' that forgetfulness, ignorance, or omission.
North:	It shows their sincerity. They quote, indeed, scarcely any poetry but Wordsworth's——for in it, above all other, their quiet, and contemplative, and meditative spirits seem to repose in delight.
Shepherd:	I canna understaun' why it should be sae, but wi' the exception o' yoursel, sir, I never kent man or woman wha loved and admired Wordsworth up to the pitch, or near till't, o' idolatrous worship, wha

	seemed to care adoit for ony ither poet, leevin or dead. He's a sectawrian, you see, sir, in the religion o' natur——
North:	Her High Priest.
Shepherd:	Weel——weel——sir, e'en be't sae. But is that ony reason why a' ither priests should be despised or disregarded, when trying in a religious speerit to expound or illustrate the same byuck——the byuck, o' natur which God has given us, wi' the haly leaves lyin open, sae that he wha rins may read, though it's only them that walks slowly, or sits down aneath the shadow o' a rock or a tree, that can understaun sufficient to privilege them to breathe forth their knowledge an' their feelings in poetry, which is aye as a prayer or a thanksgiving?
North:	The Book of the Seasons is a delightful book – and I recommend it to all lovers of nature.

THE TABLE TALK AND OMNIANA OF SAMUEL TAYLOR COLERIDGE (1772-1834), the author, with Wordsworth, of Lyrical Ballads, *and of* Kubla Khan:

14 August 1833: A Quaker is made up of ice and flame. He has no composition, no mean temperature. Hence he is rarely interested about any public measure but he becomes a fanatic, and oversteps, in his irrespective zeal, every decency and every right opposed to his course. (1896 ed. p 244)

12 January 1834: But really there is no knowing what the modern Quakers are, or believe, excepting this——that they are altogether degenerating from their ancestors of the seventeenth century. I should call modern Quakerism, so far as I know it as a scheme of faith, a Socinian Calvinism. Penn himself was a Sabellian, and seems to have disbelieved even the historical fact of the life and death of Jesus——most certainly Jesus of Nazareth was not Penn's Christ, if he had any. It is amusing to see the modern Quakers appealing now to history for a confirmation of their tenets and discipline——and by so doing, in effect abandoning the stronghold of their founders. As an *imperium in imperio,* I think the original Quakerism a conception worthy of Lycurgus. Modern Quakerism is like one of those gigantic trees which are seen in the forests of North America—— apparently flourishing, and preserving all its greatest stretch and spread of branches, but when you cut through an enormously thick and gnarled bark, you find the whole inside hollow and rotten. Modern Quakerism, like such a tree, stands upright by help of its inveterate bark alone. Bark a Quaker, and he is a poor creature. (pp 272-273)

JAPHET IN SEARCH OF A FATHER – *Captain Marryat (1792-1848)*

This novel was first published in 1836 and is the story of Japhet, a foundling, brought up in a Foundling Hospital. Being bright and quick he is eventually apprenticed to an apothecary called Phineas Cophagus, but he cannot be content with his lot and determines to set out in the world to find his father. After many adventures he is penniless and at his wits' end. He is rescued by Phineas Cophagus, who finds him unconscious in the gutter. By this time Phineas has married a Quaker and himself joined the Society. Japhet recovers his health under the care of Phineas' sister-in-law Susannah, with whom he falls in love; for her sake he decides to become a Quaker and takes to wearing Quaker dress. However, two years later he discovers that he is the son of General de Benyon and decides to take his rightful place in London society. But he cannot forget Susannah and eventually persuades her to join him and abandon her Quaker principles and plain dress. Captain Marryat's view of Quakerism is expressed in the following extract:

My dear Susannah, this is a checkered world, but not a very bad one – there is in it much of good as well as evil. The sect to which you belong avoid it – and they are unjust towards it. During the time I lived at Reading, I will cordially state to you that I met with many who called themselves of the persuasion, who were wholly unworthy of it. but they made up in outward appearance and hypocrisy what they wanted in their contact with their fellow creatures. (p 380)

Japhet goes on to point out that fashionable apparel worn by the well-to-do gives employment:

the rich should spend their money in superfluities, that the poor may be supported. Be not deceived, therefore, in future, by the outward garments, which avail nothing. (p 381)

The story ends with the marriage of Japhet and Susannah and their settling to live with General de Benyon – 'father is prettily behaved, and my Quaker wife the most fashionably dressed lady in town'.

Captain Marryat shows in this book only a superficial knowledge of Quaker principles and practice. Japhet could not, for example, simply decide to become a Quaker, even in the early 19th century. The process of joining the Society of Friends is sometimes lengthy and is taken very seriously; his so-called convincement would not be accepted. As in other Quaker women in fiction——for example in REDGAUNTLET——*Susannah is idealised as pure, sincere, beautiful and virtuous; Japhet 'felt her beauty, her purity' and 'could have worshipped her as an angel'. This sentimentalising of Quaker women has been dealt with in the introduction. There is still the suggestion that Quaker men are hypocrites, as they were considered to be a century before this novel was written.*

THE SMITH OF SMITHS, BEING THE LIFE, WIT AND HUMOUR OF SYDNEY, SMITH – ed. Hesketh Pearson, 1977(5)

Sydney Smith *(1771-1845) entered the church and eventually became canon of St Paul's. He was renowned for his wit, but his wildest extravagances were often the vehicle for sound argument:*

Mrs Fry [Elizabeth Fry] was a famous prison reformer. Sydney once accompanied her on a visit to a prison and was much touched by her humanity and the affection she inspired among the prisoners. But – 'Mrs Fry, he wrote, 'is very unpopular with the clergy; examples of living, active virtue disturb our repose, and give birth to distressing comparisons; we long to burn her alive'.

MEMOIR OF SIR THOMAS FOWELL BUXTON, 1786-1845, edited by his son Charles Buxton

Thomas Fowell Buxton *was a noted 19th-century philanthropist and played an active part in the work of the Society for the Reformation of Prison Discipline. He succeeded* William Wilberforce *as leader of the anti-slavery committee in the House of Commons and was brought into close contact with the Quaker members who were a potent force behind the activities of the committee. At some time before the autumn of 1801 he became acquainted as a youth with John, the eldest son of John Gurney★ of Earlham, near Norwich, who became a close friend. This visit to the home of his friend provides an interesting glimpse into the life of a liberal, well-to-do Quaker of the period:*

Mr Gurney had for several years been a widower. His family consisted of eleven children; three elder daughters, on the eldest of whom the charge of the rest chiefly devolved, the son whom we have mentioned, a group of four girls nearer Fowell Buxton's age, and three younger boys. He was then in his sixteenth year, and was charmed by the lively and kindly spirit which pervaded the whole party, while he was surprised at finding them all, even the younger portion of the family, zealously occupied in self-education, and full of energy in every pursuit, whether of amusement or of knowledge . . . He at once joined with them in reading and study, and from this visit may be dated a remarkable change in the whole tone

★ This was John Gurney (1749-1809) the father of Joseph John Gurney, the 19th-century evangelical minister.

of his character: he received a stimulus, not merely in the acquisition of knowledge, but in the formation of studious habits and intellectual tastes, nor could the same influence fail of extending to the refinement of his disposition and manners.

Earlham itself possessed singular charms for their young and lively party. They are described at the time of his visit as spending the fine autumn afternoons in sketching and reading under the old trees in the park, or in taking excursions, some on foot, some on horseback, into the country round; wandering homeward towards evening, with their drawings and the wild flowers they had found. The roomy old hall, also, was well fitted for the cheerful, though simple hospitalities which Mr Gurney delighted to exercise, especially towards the literary society, for which Norwich was at that time distinguished:

A characteristic anecdote of Mr Gurney has been recorded. He was a strict preserver of his game, and accordingly had an intense repugnance to everything bordering on poaching. Upon one occasion, when walking in his park, he heard a shot fired in a neighbouring wood – he hurried to the spot, and his naturally placid temper was considerably ruffled on seeing a young officer with a pheasant at his feet, deliberately reloading his gun. As the young man, however, replied to his rather warm expressions by a polite apology, Mr Gurney's wrath was somewhat allayed; but he could not refrain from asking the intruder what he would do, if he caught a man trespassing on his premises. 'I would ask him to luncheon,' was the reply. The serenity of this impudence was not to be resisted. Mr Gurney not only invited him to luncheon, but supplied him with dogs and a gamekeeper, and secured him excellent sport for the remainder of the day.

Mr Gurney belonged to the Society of Friends; but his family was not brought up with any strict regard to its peculiarities. He put little restraint on the domestic amusements; and music and dancing were among their favourite recreations . . .

Thomas Fowell Buxton freely acknowledged the important part played by the Society in the anti-slavery movement, as the two following extracts show:

Anti-slavery operations were now commenced with vigour, and for some time all went on well. Dr Lushington, Lord Suffield, and several others, who had taken a prominent part in the reformation of Prison Discipline, now threw all their energies into this new undertaking. Early in March Mr. Wilberforce published his well-known 'Appeal on behalf of the slaves'. At about the same time the Anti-Slavery Society was formed (Mr Buxton being appointed a Vice-President), and the Committee engaged warmly in the task of collecting evidence and spreading information through the country. Public feeling was soon roused into activity, and petitions began to flow in; the lead was taken by the Society of Friends, and it was determined that the presentation of their appeal by the hands of Mr. Wilberforce should be the opening of the parliamentary campaign. He introduced it by saying that a similar petition which he had had the honour of presenting nearly thirty years before, had been the first effort against the kindred iniquity of the Slave Trade, and that in presenting this one 'he considered that the first stone was laid of an edifice which would stand at some future period, an ornament to the land'. (1823)

A few days later, in presenting, among 500 petitions against slavery, one subscribed by the Society of Friends, he said:–

'I have great pleasure in presenting this petition from that body; as they were the very first persons in the country who promulgated the doctrine that the buying, selling, or holding of slaves was contrary to the Christian religion. Forty years ago they presented the first petition for the abolition of the slave-trade, and eight years ago they presented the first petition for the abolition of slavery.' (1831)

SHIRLEY – Charlotte Brontë (1816-1855)

This novel, which was first published in 1849, is set in Yorkshire in the first decade of the 18th century, the early years of the industrial revolution. A central theme is the hostility caused by the arrival of new machinery at a mill for weaving cloth, which will inevitably throw men out of work and cause great hardship. The book contains a description of a violent attack on the mill by enraged mill workers, typical of scenes all over the north of England at that time. But the mill-owner himself is in straitened circumstances, caused by the 'Orders in Council' which during the Napoleonic Wars *prohibited trade with the continent of Europe. Neither of the two contrasting heroines, the friends* Shirley and Caroline, *is a* Quaker, *but there are several references to* Quakers *in the book and it is clear that* Charlotte Brontë *understood Quaker ways and sometimes approved of them. She does, however, compare Quaker quietness not altogether favourably with Wesleyans:*

Briar Chapel, a large, new, raw Wesleyan place of worship, rose but a hundred yards distant; and, as there was even now a prayer-meeting being held within its walls, the illumination of its windows cast a bright reflection on the road, while a hymn of a most extraordinary description, such as a very Quaker might feel himself moved by the spirit to dance to, roused cheerily all the echoes of the vicinage.

Charlotte Brontë contrasts the brilliant and lively Shirley with the quiet Caroline:

This question was a specimen of one of Shirley's sharp, sudden turns: Caroline used to be fluttered by them at first, but she had now got into the way of parrying these home-thrusts like a little Quakeress.

Caroline is dressing for the Whitsuntide fête and reflects that:

After all, she was an imperfect, faulty human being; fair enough of form, hue, and array; but as Cyril Hall said, neither so good nor so great as the withered Miss Ainley, now putting on her best black gown and Quaker-drab shawl and bonnet in her narrow cottage-chamber.

The character of an Irish curate who settles in Yorkshire:

Being human, of course he had his faults; these, however, were proper, steady-going, clerical faults; what many would call virtues: the circumstance of finding himself invited to tea with a dissenter would unhinge him for a week; the spectacle of a Quaker wearing his hat in the church . . . these things could make strange havoc of Mr Macarthey's physical and mental economy; otherwise he was sane and rational, diligent and charitable.

Charlotte Brontë was of course a clergyman's daughter, but in her portrayal of the character of Mr Macarthey she suggests his prejudice to be both irrational and uncharitable. Perhaps she had met such views among the curates who came to assist her father.

JOHN TREGENOWETH HIS MARK – Mark Guy Pearse, c.1850

John Tregenoweth of the title of this book is a Cornishman blinded in a mining accident. After some time spent vainly trying to earn a living playing his fiddle round the streets of the little Cornish town where he lives, he takes to drink and becomes completely penniless, even selling his fiddle. He signs the pledge and then decides to seek the help of the one man he feels may take pity on him, a Quaker. The following extract describes his encounter with the Quaker:

There was only one gentleman I could think of who was likely to do anything for me, so all of a tremble and flutter I made for his house and knocked on the door.

I could tell from the way he spoke to me at first that he had heard all about me, and my heart sank to my shoes. Yet I felt that he was the one man in the world that I could trust, and so I told him all the story, and how I had signed the pledge, and meant to keep it too.

His tone altered then, and he spoke a good deal kinder after that. He asked me what I was going to do for a living; so I said that I'd been thinking if I could get a few shillings I might buy back my fiddle. He sat quiet for a long time, and then he said,

'Nay, my friend, the fiddle is gone, and a good thing too. It would always be a temptation to thee, John——always a snare.'

Well, that seemed to knock my only hope clear out of me; so, vexed that I had come, I rose to go away.

'Sit down, Friend, sit down,' says he, in his quiet way.

I put down my hat and stood by the chair, but I hadn't heart enough to care for anything he could say.

He was quiet again for a long time, and then he began, very slowly and quietly.

'John, I've been thinkin' if thou hast a donkey and cart it would help thee. Thy daughter Mary could lead it to the beach, and thou could'st fill it with sand and go from door to door, selling it to thy neighbours.' [*For the floors of their houses.*]

'Me have a donkey and cart, Sir!' I cried out; 'why, I might as well think about a carriage and pair.'

'I think we can manage it for thee, Friend,' says he, so quiet as ever.

He got out a paper, and wrote something down that he read to me, and told me to take it round and see what I could get; and he put down his own name for a'most enough to buy the donkey, and said, moreover, that he should lend me five shillings for the time.

I couldn't thank him, – my heart was too full; but I could a'most have worshipped him then and there.

The Quaker also gives John an old coat, which he so greatly venerates that he attributes a visionary experience to the fact that he was wearing it at the time. The Quaker finally asks John whether he ever goes to the 'House of God'. John is afraid he will be expected to attend a Quaker meeting, but the Friend is satisfied that he should worship with the Primative Methodists, as he used to do – 'The very place for thee, John; go there, and the Lord bless thee'. The Quaker's faith in John is justified; he mends his ways and prospers. In this episode Mark Guy Pearse shows a true understanding of the basis of philanthropy. The Quaker will not give John money which would only tide him over his difficulties temporarily; instead, he puts him in the way of helping himself, enabling him to earn a living for the rest of his days.

LAVENGRO – George Borrow (1803-1881)

This book, which was first published in 1851, is subtitled 'The Scholar——The Gypsy——The Priest' and recounts George Borrow's experiences among the gypsies during one of his long journeys. The chapter from which the following extract is taken is devoted to a discussion between an old man and his young companion on the subject of suicide. The old man remembers a Quaker suicide as follows:

I remember a female Quaker who committed suicide by cutting her throat, but she did it decorously and decently: kneeling down over a pail, so that not one drop fell upon the floor, thus exhibiting in her last act that sense of neatness for which Quakers are distinguished. I have always had a respect for that woman's memory.

WILD WAYS by George Borrow – his account of a journey through Wales in 1854:

Shortly afterwards meeting a man I asked him how far it was to Caefili.

'When you come to the Quakers' Yard, which is a little farther on, you will be seven miles from Caerfili.'

'What is the Quakers' Yard?'

'A place where the people called Quakers bury their dead.'

'Is there a village near it?'

'There is, and the village is called by the same name.'

'Are there any Quakers in it?'

'Not one, nor in the neighbourhood, but there are some, I believe, in Cardiff.'

'Why do they bury their dead there?'

'You should ask them, not me. I know nothing about them, and don't want; they are a bad sort of people.'

'Did they ever do you any harm?'

'Can't say they did. Indeed I never saw one in the whole of my life.'

'Then why do you call them bad?'

'Because everybody says they are.'

'Not everybody. I don't; I have always found them the salt of the earth.'

'Then it is salt that has lost its savour. But perhaps you are one of them?'

'No I belong to the Church of England.'

'Oh, you do. Then goodnight to you. I am a Methodist. I thought at first that you were one of our ministers, and had hoped to hear from you something profitable and conducive to salvation, but——'

'Well, so you shall. Never speak ill of people of whom you know nothing. If that isn't a saying conducive to salvation, I know not what is. Good evening to you.'

I soon reached the village. Singular enough, the people of the very first house, at which I inquired about the Quakers' Yard, were entrusted with the care of it. On my expressing a wish to see it, a young woman took down a key, and said that if I would follow her she would show it me. The Quakers' burying place is situated on a little peninsula or tongue of land, having a brook on its eastern and northern sides, and on its western the Taf. It is a little oblong yard, with low walls, partly overhung with ivy. The entrance is a porch to the south. The Quakers are no friends to tombstones, and the only visible evidence that this was a place of burial was a single flag-stone, with a half obliterated inscription, which with some difficulty I deciphered, and was as follows:–

To the Memory of Thomas Edmunds
Who died April the ninth 1802 aged 60 years.
And of Mary Edmunds
Who died January the fourth 1810 aged 70

The beams of the descending sun gilded the Quakers' burial-ground as I trod its precincts. A lovely resting-place looked that little oblong yard on the peninsula, by the confluence of the waters, and quite in keeping with the character of the Christian people who sleep within it. The Quakers have for some time past been a decaying sect, but they have done good work in their day, and when they are extinct they are not destined to be soon forgotten. Soon forgotten! How should such a sect ever be forgotten, to which have belonged three such men as George Fox, William Penn and Joseph Gurney?

JOHN ENDICOTT – Henry Wadsworth Longfellow (1807-1882)

This poetic drama in five acts, published about the middle of the century, is the first of the New England Tragedies. It is set in Boston in the year 1665 and its subject is the persecution of the Quakers by the Puritans. The Governer, John Endicott the elder, is determined to enforce the laws against the Quakers; the heart of his son John is softened towards them and he falls in love with the young Quaker girl Edith. His father casts him off in anger. Towards the end of the drama a Mandamus arrives from Charles II directing that all the Quakers should be freed and that persecution should cease. Coming on top of the loss of his son, this it too much for Governor Endicott, whose death closes the poem. In the verses quoted below, it is Sunday afternoon in the Meeting-house. The Puritan John Norton is in the pulpit, with Governor Endicott in a canopied seat, attended by four halberdiers. Norton's sermon is halted by the entry of Edith and the Quakers:

Edith, barefooted and clad in sackcloth, with her hair hanging loose upon her shoulders, walks slowly up the aisle, followed by Wharton and other Quakers. The congregation starts up in confusion.

Edith: (*to Norton, raising her hand*). Peace!

Norton: Anathema maranatha!
        The Lord cometh!

Edith: Yea, verily he cometh,
        and shall judge
        The shepherds of Israel, who do
        feed themselves,

And leave their flocks to eat what
    they have trodden
Beneath their feet.

Norton: Be silent, babbling woman!
St Paul commands all women to
    keep silence
Within the churches.

Edith: Yet women prayed
And prophesied at Corinth in his
    day;
And among those on whom the
    fiery tongues
Of Pentecost descended, some
    were women!

Norton: The Elders of the
Churches, by our law,
Alone have power to open the doors
    of speech
And silence in the Assembly. I
    command you!

Edith: The law of God is greater
    than your laws!
Ye build your church with blood,
    your town with crime;
The heads thereof give judgment
    for reward;
The priests thereof teach only for
    their hire;
Your laws condemn the innocent
    to death;
And against this I bear my
    testimony.

Norton: What testimony?
Edith: That of the
        Holy Spirit,
Which, as your Calvin says,
    surpasseth reason.

Norton: The labourer is worthy
    of his hire.

Edith: Yet our great Master
        did not teach for hire,
And the Apostles without purse or
    scrip

Went forth to do his work. Behold
this box
Beneath thy pulpit. Is it for the
poor?
Thou canst not answer. It is for
the Priest;
And against this I bear my
testimony.

Norton: Away with all these
Heretics and Quakers!
Quakers, forsooth! Because
quaking fell
On Daniel, at beholding of the
Vision,
Must ye needs shake and quake?
Because Isaiah
Went stripped and barefoot, must
ye wail and howl?
Must ye go stripped and naked?
must ye make
A wailing like the dragons, and
mourning
As of the owls? Ye verify the adage
That Satan is God's ape! away
with them!

MOBY DICK, OR THE WHITE WHALE – *Herman Melville (1819-1891)*

*This story, which was published in 1851, is told in the first person by a character
known only as* Ishmael, *the wanderer. He has a great longing to see the world and finds
himself in Nantucket, about to sail as a deck hand in the* 'Pequod', *a whaling ship under
the command of* Captain Ahab. *Ishmael is taken aboard the 'Pequod' by one of the
owners,* Captain Peleg, *in order to sign the necessary papers; a co-owner of the 'Pequod'
is* Captain Bildad. *The following extract introduces the Quaker whale hunters of
Nantucket:*

Now Bildad, like Peleg, and indeed many other Nantucketers, was a Quaker,
the island having been originally settled by that sect; and to this day its inhabitants in general retain in an uncommon measure the peculiarities of the Quaker,

only variously and anomously modified by things altogether alien and hetero-geneous. For some of these Quakers are the most sanguinary of all sailors and whale-hunters. They are fighting Quakers: they are Quakers with a vengeance.

So that there are some instances among them of men, who, named with Scripture names——a singularly common fashion on the island——and in child-hood naturally imbibing the stately dramatic thee and thou of Quaker idiom; still, from the audacious, daring, and boundless adventure of their subsequent lives, strangely blend with these outgrown peculiarities, a thousand bold dashes of character, not unworthy of a Scandinavian sea-king, or a poetical pagan Roman. And when these things unite in a man of greatly superior natural force, with a globular brain and a ponderous heart; who has also by the stillness and seclusion of many long night-watches in the remotest waters, and beneath constel-lations never seen here in the north, been led to think untraditionally and inde-pendently; receiving all nature's sweet or savage impressions fresh from her own virgin voluntary and confiding breast, and thereby chiefly, but with some help from accidental advantages, to learn a bold and nervous lofty language——that man makes one in a whole nation's census——a mighty pageant creature, formed for noble tragedies. Nor will it at all detract from him, dramatically regarded, if either by birth or other circumstances, he have what seems a half wilful over-ruling morbidness at the bottom of his nature. For all men tragically great are made so through a certain morbidness . . . But as yet we have not to do with such an one, but with quite another; and still a man, who, if indeed peculiar, it only results again from another phase of the Quaker, modified by individual circumstances.

Like Captain Peleg, Captain Bildad was a well-to-do, retired whaleman. But unlike Captain Peleg——who cared not a rush for what was called serious things, and indeed deemed those self-same serious things the veriest of all trifles—— Captain Bildad had not only been originally educated according to the strictest sect of Nantucket Quakerism, but all his subsequent ocean life, and the sight of many unclad, lovely island creatures, round the Horn——all that had not moved this native born Quaker one single jot, had not so much altered one angle of his vest. Still, for all this immutableness, was there some lack of common consistency about worthy Captain Bildad. Though refusing, from conscientious scruples, to bear arms against land invaders, yet himself had illimitably invaded the Atlantic and Pacific; and though a sworn foe to human bloodshed, yet had he in his straight-bodied coat, spilled tuns upon tuns of leviathan gore. How now in the contemplative evening of his days, the pious Bildad reconciled these things in the reminiscence, I do not know; but it did not seem to concern him much, and very probably he had long since come to the sage and sensible conclusion that a man's religion is one thing, and this practical world quite another. This world pays dividends. Rising from a little cabin-boy in short clothes of the drabbest drab, to a harpooneer in a broad shad-bellied waistcoat; from that becoming boatheader, chief mate, and captain, and finally a ship owner; Bildad, as I hinted before, had concluded his adventurous career by wholly retiring from active life at the goodly age of sixty, and dedicating his remaining days to the quiet receiving of his well-earned income.

Now Bildad, I am sorry to say, had the reputation of being an incorrigible old hunks, and in his sea-going days, a bitter, hard task-master. They told me in Nantucket, though it certainly seems a curious story, that when he sailed the old *Categut* whaleman, his crew upon arriving home, were mostly all carried ashore to the hospital, sore exhausted and worn out. For a pious man, especially a Quaker, he was certainly rather hard-hearted, to say the least. He never used to swear, though, at his men, they said; but somehow he got an inordinate quantity of cruel, unmitigated hard work out of them. When Bildad was chief-mate, to have his drab-coloured eye intently looking at you, made you feel completely nervous, till you could clutch at something——a hammer or a marling-spike, and go to work like a man, at something or other, never mind what. Indolence and idleness perished before him. His own person was the exact embodiment of his utilitarian character. On his long, gaunt body, he carried no spare flesh, no superfluous beard, his chin having a soft, economical nap to it, like the worn nap of his broad-brimmed hat.

Such then, was the person that I saw seated on the transom when I followed Captain Peleg down into the cabin. The space between the decks was small; and there, bolt upright, sat old Bildad, who always sat so, and never leaned, and this to save his coat-tails. His broad-brim was placed beside him; his legs were stiffly crossed; his drab vesture was buttoned up to his chin; and spectacles on nose, he seemed absorbed in reading from a ponderous volume. 'Bildad,' cried Captain Peleg, 'at it again, Bildad, eh? Ye have been studying those Scriptures, now, for the last thirty years, to my certain knowledge. How far ye got, Bildad?'

As if long habituated to such profane talk from his old ship-mate, Bildad, without noticing his present irreverence, quietly looked up, and seeing me, glanced again enquiringly towards Peleg.

'He says he's our man, Bildad,' said Peleg, 'he wants to ship.'

'Dost thee?' said Bildad, in a hollow tone, and turning round to me.

'I dost,' said I, unconsciously, he was so intense a Quaker.

'What do ye think of him, Bildad?' said Peleg.

'He'll do,' said Bildad, and then went on spelling away at his book in a mumbling tone quite audible.

I thought him the queerest old Quaker I ever saw, especially as Peleg, his friend and old shipmate, seemed such a blusterer.

MAUD – Alfred Lord Tennyson (1809-1892)

MAUD was published in 1855, in the middle of the Crimean War. The verses quoted reveal Tennyson's bitterness towards the Quaker peace testimony and his view of Quakers as traders, only interested in their profits. This view has been met with earlier, in Cobbett:

Part I, X iii

Last week came one to the county town,
To preach our poor little army down,
And play the game of the despot kings,
Tho' the state has done it and thrice as
    well:
This broad-brimm'd hawker of holy
    things.
Whose ear is cramm'd with his cotton,
    and rings
Even in dreams to the chink of his pence,
This huckster put down war! can he tell
Whether war be a cause or a consequence?
Put down the passions that make earth
    Hell!
Down with ambition, avarice, pride,
Jealousy, down! cut off from the mind
The bitter springs of anger and fear;
Down too, down at your own fireside,
With the evil tongue and the evil ear,
For each is at war with mankind.

Part II, V x

Friend, to be struck by the public foe,
Then to strike him and lay him low,
That were a public merit, far,
Whatever the Quaker holds, from sin;
But the red life split for a private blow –
I swear to you, lawful and lawless war
Are scarcely even akin.

JOHN HALIFAX, GENTLEMAN – Dinah Maria Mulock (Mrs Craik) (1826-1887)

This novel, which was published in 1857, is set in the early years of the 19th century and shows little understanding of Quaker principles. Mrs Craik has used the Quaker conceptions of justice and honesty in order to present the Quaker Abel Fletcher as stern and uncompromising, showing neither compassion nor understanding in his dealings with people. He is never shown as attending a meeting for worship nor as having heard of George Fox's injunction to look for that of God in every man. His son Phineas, a sickly boy of 16 when the story opens, finds a friend and companion in John Halifax, who as a destitute lad looking for work is taken on by Fletcher to work in his tannery, but only after the strictest enquiries as to his honesty and his past. His wages were fixed at three shillings a week, a sum which has to provide both food and lodging, but Fletcher is shown as sharing the view that 'plenty was not good for the working classes, they required to be kept low'. *John Halifax soon proves his worth both as an employee and friend and Phineas, the narrator of the story, clings to him as David to his Jonathan, his sole contact with the outside world.*

Mrs Craik *depicts Abel Fletcher as a strict Quaker to whom theatre-going was an abomination. John and Phineas are persuaded by a group of strolling players to visit a performance of MACBETH, which is of course no crime as far as John is concerned. The punishment meted out by Abel Fletcher, who sees John as leading his son into evil ways, is that the friendship which means so much to Phineas is in future forbidden and John's prospects of advancement to an apprenticeship and eventual partnership in the business are at an end.*

Abel Fletcher's unyielding nature and insistence on what Mrs Craik regards as Quaker principles of right and justice are further depicted in an episode when both his life and property are in jeopardy. This year 1800 was known as the 'dear year'. *Harvests had failed and the price of corn was increasing. Abel, who had acquired a grain mill in addition to his tannery, was busy buying up corn, but before he decided to sell it the starving crowd, many of whom had had no food for themselves and their families for some days, began to riot and storm the mill. The mob shouted to him to throw down the corn, to which in ungovernable anger he replied,* 'Abel Fletcher will throw it down to ye, ye knaves,' *and flung the precious wheat into the river. It is John Halifax who has to rescue him from the anger of the rioters.*

The story's main interest lies in the fortunes of John Halifax and his eventual marriage to the heroine Ursula March. Abel Fletcher dies about halfway through the novel, having served the author's purpose in high-lighting the good and admirable qualities bestowed upon the hero, John Halifax.

THE QUAKERS' MEETING – *Samuel Lover (1797-1868)*

Samuel Lover *was an Irish novelist, playwright and song-writer. He is remembered for his ballad, and the novel which developed from it,* RORY O'MORE. *This novel deals with the great rebellion in Ireland of 1798, in which Irish Quakers suffered great hardship, some losing all they possessed in the tragedy which overwhelmed the country.* THE QUAKERS' MEETING *was published in 1857:*

A TRAVELLER wended the wilds among,
With a purse of gold and a silver tongue;
His hat it was broad and all drab were his clothes,
For he hated high colours – except on the nose.
And he met with a lady, the story goes.
    Heigho! yea thee and nay thee.

The damsel she cast him a beamy blink,
And the traveller nothing was loth, I think,
Her merry black eye beamed her bonnet beneath,
And the quaker he grinned, for he'd very good teeth,
And he ask'd 'Art thee going to ride on the heath?'
    Heigho! yea thee and nay thee.

'I hope you'll protect me kind sir,' said the maid,
'As to ride this heath over I'm sadly afraid;
For robbers, they say, here in numbers abound,
And I wouldn't 'for anything' I should be found,
For – between you and me – I have five hundred pound.'
    Heigho! yea thee and nay thee.

'If that is thee own dear,' the quaker he said,
'I ne'er saw a maiden I sooner would wed;
And I have another five hundred just now,
In the padding that's under my saddle bow,
And I'll settle it all upon thee, I vow!'
    Heigho! yea thee and nay thee.

The maiden she smiled, and her rein she drew,
'Your offer I'll take – though I'd not take you.'
A pistol she held at the quaker's head –
'Now give me your gold – or I'll give you my lead –
Tis under the saddle I think you said.'
    Heigho! yea thee and nay thee.

The damsel she ripped up the saddle-bow,
And the quaker was never a quaker till now,
And he saw, by the fair one he wish'd for a bride,
His purse borne away with a swaggering stride,
And the eye that shamm'd tender, now only defied.
    Heigho! yea thee and nay thee.

'The spirit doth move me, friend Broadbrim,' quoth she,
'To take all this filthy temptation from thee,
For mammon deceiveth – and beauty is fleeting;
Accept from thy maid'n a right loving greeting,
For much doth she profit by this Quaker's meeting.'
    Heigho! yea thee and nay thee.

'And hark! jolly quaker, so rosy and sly,
Have righteousness, more than a wench in thine eye,
Don't go again peeping girls' bonnets beneath,
Remember the one you met on the heath –
Her name's Jimmy Barlow – I tell to your teeth!'
    Heigho! yea thee and nay thee.

'Friend James,' quoth the quaker, 'pray listen to me,
For thou cans't confer a great favour, d'ye see;
The gold thou hast taken is not mine, my friend,
But my master's – and truly on thee I depend,
To make it appear I my trust did defend.'
    Heigho! yea thee and nay thee.

'So fire a few shots through my clothes, here and there,
To make it appear 'twas a desp'rate affair.' –
So Jim he popped first through the skirt of his coat,
And then through his collar – quite close to his throat,
'Now one through my broadbrim,' quoth Ephraim, 'I vote.'
    Heigho! yea thee and nay thee.

'I have but a brace,' said bold Jim, 'and they're spent,
And I won't load again for a make-believe rent.'——
'Then'——said Ephraim, producing his pistols——'just give
My five hundred pounds back——or as sure as you live
I'll make of your body a riddle or sieve.
    Heigho! yea thee and nay thee.

Jim Barlow was diddled——and, though he was game,
He saw Ephraim's pistol so deadly in aim,
That he gave up the gold, and he took to his scrapers,
And when the whole story got into the papers,
They said that 'the thieves were no match for the Quakers'.
    Heigho! yea thee and nay thee.

This story, which was published in 1863, is set in Monkshaven (Whitby in Yorkshire) in 1793, when most men there worked in the whaling trade, a profitable but dangerous occupation. A threat worse than the sea, however, was the pressgang. The war against revolutionary France had just started, sailors were urgently needed in the fighting ships and so able-bodied young men were kidnapped as they returned from whaling voyages or went about their business. They often had to serve for many years and some returned wounded or died in battle.

In contrast to these violent events two elderly Quaker brothers, John and Jeremiah Foster, keep a flourishing shop in Monkshaven, half grocery, half drapery and, though upright Friends, do not think it wrong to sell smuggled goods. One of their assistants, Philip Hepburn, is in love with Sylvia, the pretty only daughter of local farmer Daniel Robson, a strong-minded Yorkshireman. Sylvia scorns the sober Philip and falls in love with the more romantic Charley Kincaid, a 'specksioneer' (harpooner) on a whaling vessel. The novel is principally concerned with Sylvia's eventual marriage to Philip. The following extract gives Mrs Gaskell's view of late 18th-century Quakers:

Foster's shop was the shop of Monkshaven. It was kept by two quaker brothers, who were now old men; and their father had kept it before them; and probably his father before that. People remembered it was an old-fashioned dwelling-house, with a sort of supplementary shop with unglazed windows projecting from the lower story. These had long been filled with panes of glass that at the present day would be accounted very small, but which seventy years ago were much admired for their size . . . Half the shop was appropriated to grocery; the other half to drapery, and a little mercery. The good old brothers gave all their customers a kindly welcome; shaking hands with many of them, and asking all after their families and domestic circumstances before proceeding to business. They would not for the world have had any sign of festivity at Christmas, and scrupulously kept their shop open at that holy festival, ready themselves to serve sooner than tax the consciences of any of their assistants, only nobody ever came. But on New Year's Day they had a great cake, and wine, ready in the parlour behind the shop, of which all who came in to buy anything were asked to partake. Yet, though scrupulous in most things, it did not go against the consciences of these two good brothers to purchase smuggled articles. There was a back way from the river side, up a covered entry, to the yard-door of the Fosters, and a peculiar kind of knock at this door always brought out either John or Jeremiah, or if not them, their shopman, Philip Hepburn; and the same cake and wine that the excise officer's wife might just have been tasting, was brought out in the back parlour to treat the smugglers. There was a little locking of doors, and drawing of the green silk curtain that was supposed to shut out the shop, but really all this was done very much for form's sake. Everybody in Monkshaven smuggled who could, and great reliance was placed on the excise officer's neighbourly feelings.

The story went that John and Jeremiah Foster were so rich that they could buy up all the new town across the bridge. They had certainly begun to have a kind of primitive bank in connection with their shop, receiving and taking care of such money as people did not wish to retain in their houses for fear of burglars. No one asked them for interest on the money thus deposited, nor did they give any; but, on the other hand, if any of their customers, on whose character they could depend, wanted a little advance, the Fosters, after all the enquiries made, and in some cases due security given, were not unwilling to lend a moderate sum without charging a penny for the use of their money. All the articles they sold were as good as they knew how to choose, and for them they expected and obtained ready money. It was said they only kept the shop for their amusement.

THE WESTMINSTER REVIEW, July 1869: from an article by Edgar Sheppard, M.D.

I was assured the other day of the fact by a very intelligent physician who practised among them [*Quakers*] for twenty years and who informs me that few of the richer sort live to be fifty, but die of a sort of atrophy, their cold blood just stagnating by degrees among their fat. The affection is known in this part of the country [*Liverpool*] by the name of 'Quaker's disease', and more than half of them go out so.

STATISTICAL INQUIRY INTO THE EFFICACY OF PRAYER – Francis Galton (1822-1911)

This inquiry was published in 1872 and is concerned with the problem of fixed annuity rates and insurance company profits. It has been used by Peter Brian Medawar *in his book INDUCTION AND INTUITION IN SCIENTIFIC THOUGHT, 1969, who points out that* 'the rates offered by different companies are competitive and must be judiciously worked out'[6]:

It would be most unwise, from a business point of view, to allow the devout, supposing their greater longevity even probable, to obtain annuities at the same rate as the profane, Before insurance offices accept a life, they make confidential enquiries into the antecedents of the applicant. But such a question has never been heard of as 'Does he habitually use family prayers and private devotions?' Insurance offices, so wakeful to sanatory influences, absolutely ignore prayer as one of them. The same is true for insurances of all descriptions, as those connected with fire, ships, lightning, hail, accidental death, and cattle sickness. How is it possible to explain why Quakers who are most devout and shrewd men of business, have ignored these considerations, except on the ground that they do not really believe in what they and others freely assert about the efficacy of prayer?

THE GREY BRETHREN – Michael Fairless (1869-1901)

Michael Fairless *was the pen-name of* Margaret Fairless Barber. *She trained as a nurse, but her health broke down while she was in her twenties. All three of her books were published posthumously,* THE GREY BRETHREN, *which had previously been published in* THE COMMONWEALTH, *in 1905:*

Some of the happiest memories of my childhood are of days spent in a little Quaker colony on a high hill.

The walk was in itself a preparation, for the hill was long and steep and at the mercy of the north-east wind; but at the top, sheltered by a copse and a few tall trees, stood a small house, reached by a flagged pathway skirting one side of a bright trim garden.

I, with my seven summers of lonely, delicate childhood, felt, when I gently closed the gate behind me, that I shut myself into Peace. The house was always somewhat dark, and there were no domestic sounds. The two old ladies, sisters, both born in the last century, sat in the cool, dim parlour, netting or sewing. Rebecca was small, with a nutcracker nose and chin; Mary, tall and dignified, needed no velvet under the net cap. I can feel now the touch of the cool dove-coloured silk against my cheek, as I sat on the floor, watching the nimble fingers with the shuttle, and listened as Mary read aloud a letter received that morning, describing a meeting of the faithful and the 'moving of the Spirit' among them. I had a mental picture of the 'Holy Heavenly Dove', with its wings of silvery grey, hovering over my dear old ladies; and I doubt not my vision was a true one.

Once as I watched Benjamin, the old gardener——a most 'stiff-backed Friend' despite his stoop and his seventy years——putting scarlet geraniums and yellow fever-few in the centre bed, I asked, awe-struck, whether such glowing colours were approved; Rebecca smiled and said——'Child, dost thee not think the Lord may have his glories?' and I looked from the living robe of scarlet and gold to the dove-coloured gown, and said: 'Would it be pride in thee to wear his glories?' and Mary answered for her——'The change is not yet; better beseems us the ornament of a meek and quiet spirit.'. . .

A city of Peace, this little house, for the same severely-gentle decorum reigned in the kitchen as elsewhere: and now, where is haunt to be found?

In the earlier part of this century the Friends bore a most important witness. They were a standing rebuke to rough manners, rude speech, and to the too often mere outward show of religion. No one could fail to be impressed by the atmosphere of peace suggested by their bearing and presence; and the gentle sheltered, contemplative lives lived by most of them undoubtedly made them unusually responsive to spiritual influence. Now, the young birds have left the parent nest and the sober plumage and soft speech; they are as other men; and in a few short years the word Quaker will sound as strange in our ears as the older appellation Shaker does now . . .

We of the outward and visible covenant need them, with their inherited mysticism, ordered contemplation, and spiritual vision; we need them for ourselves . . .

THE KINGDOM OF GOD IS WITHIN YOU – Leo Tolstoy (1828-1910)

In his preface to this book Tolstoy refers to a book he wrote in 1884, called WHAT I BELIEVE, *which gives an account of his belief and includes the following passage:*

Like most people, I knew very little of what had previously been done and preached and written on the subject of non-resistance to evil. I knew what had been said on the subject by the Fathers of the Church – Origen, Tertullian, and others – and I knew that the so-called sects of Mennonites, Herrnhuters, and Quakers, who do not allow a Christian to use weapons, and do not accept military service, have existed and still exist; but of what these so-called sects have done towards elucidating this question I knew but little.

The first section of THE KINGDOM OF GOD, *published in 1893, in which Tolstoy treats the subject of non-violence, opens with a tribute to Quaker views on the unlawfulness of war and the use of violence for a Christian. He develops this theme in the following extracts:*

Among the first responses to my book [*that of 1884*] were letters from American Quakers. In those letters, expressing their sympathy with my views as to the unlawfulness of war or the use of violence for a Christian, the Quakers gave me details of their so-called sect, which for more than two hundred years has professed and practised the teaching of Christ as to non-resistance of evil by violence, and does not make use of weapons in self-defence. Together with these letters the Quakers sent me their pamphlets, journals, and books, from which I learnt how, already many years ago, they had irrefutably demonstrated that it is a Christian's duty to fulfil the command of not resisting evil by violence, and how fully they had exposed the error of the Church's teaching which allows of capital punishment and war.

Having proved by a whole series of arguments and texts that a religion based on peacefulness and goodwill towards men is incompatible with war——that is, with mutilating and killing men——the Quakers maintain and prove that nothing has contributed so much to obscure Christian truth in the eyes of the heathen, or has so hindered the spread of Christianity in the world, as the sanctioning and practice of war and violence by Christians . . . (p 3)

The activity of W. L. Garrison in founding the Society of Non-Resistance, and his Declaration, more even than my relation with the Quakers, convinced me that State Christianity's abandonment of Christ's law of non-resistance by violence had been observed and pointed out long ago, and that men have laboured and still labour to expose it . . .

A fourth and yet more ingenious way in which people deal with the question of a Christian's attitude towards Christ's commandment not to resist evil by violence, consists in declaring that they do not deny the commandment but recognize it like all the others, only they do not ascribe any special and exclusive significance to it as the sectarians do. To regard this command as an invariable condition of Christian life, as Garrison, Ballon, Dymond, the Quakers, the Mennonites, and the Shakers do, and as the Moravian Brethren, the Waldenses, the Albigenses, the Bogomites, and the Paulicians did in the past, is one-sided sectarianism. This command has neither more nor less importance than any other and a man who through weakness infringes any of the commandments, including that of non-resistance, does not therefore cease to be a Christian, provided that he holds the true faith. (p 44)

CHAPTER IV

The Twentieth Century

THE VARIETIES OF RELIGIOUS EXPERIENCE – William James (1842-1910)

This book was first published in 1902. In the first extract William James is concerned with religious genius and nervous instability:

Even more perhaps than other kinds of genius, religious leaders have been subject to abnormal psychical visitations. Invariably they have been creatures of exalted emotional sensibility. Often they have led a discordant inner life, and had melancholy during a part of their career. They have known no measure, been liable to obsessions and fixed ideas; and frequently they have fallen into trances, heard voices, seen visions, and presented all sorts of peculiarities which are ordinarily classed as pathological. Often, moreover, these pathological features in their career have helped to give them their religious authority and influence.

If you ask for a concrete example, there can be no better one than is furnished by the person of George Fox. The Quaker religion which he founded is something which it is impossible to overpraise. In a day of shams, it was a religion of veracity rooted in spiritual inwardness, and a return to something more like the original gospel truth than men had ever known in England. So far as our Christian sects are to-day evolving into liberality, they are simply reverting in essence to the position which Fox and the early Quakers so long ago assumed. No one can pretend for a moment that in point of spiritual sagacity, Fox's mind was unsound. Every one who confronted him personally, from Oliver Cromwell down to county magistrates and jailers, seems to have acknowledged his superior power. Yet from the point of view of his nervous constitution, Fox was a psychopath or détraqué of the deepest dye. (pp 6-7)

The ascetic forms which the impulse for veracity and purity of life may take are often pathetic enough. The early Quakers, for example, had hard battles to wage against the worldliness and insincerity of the ecclesiastical Christianity of their time. Yet the battle that cost them most wounds was probably that which they fought in defense of their own right to social veracity and sincerity in their thee-ing and thou-ing, in not doffing the hat or giving titles of respect. It was laid on George Fox that these conventional customs were a lie and a sham, and the whole body of his followers thereupon renounced them, as a sacrifice to truth, and so that their acts and the spirit they professed might be more in accord (pp 291-292).

THE EVERLASTING MERCY – John Masefield (1878-1967)

Saul Kane, *the narrator of the poem, which was published in 1911, is a ne'er-do-well, poacher, thief, drunkard and womaniser. He gets into a fight with an old friend and afterwards drinks himself until sodden with a group of cronies. A mother accuses him of callousness and leading the young astray, which for the first time causes him to question his way of life. Finally, he is rescued by a Quakeress:*

There used to be a custom then,
Miss Bourne, the Friend, went round at ten
To all the pubs in all the place
To bring the drunkard's soul to grace;
Some sulked, of course, and some were stirred,
But none gave her a dirty word.
A tall pale woman, grey and bent,
Folk said of her that she was sent.
She wore Friend's clothes, and women smiled,
But she'd a heart just like a child.
She come to see us closing time
When we were at some smutty rhyme,
And I was mad and ripe for fun;
So when she come so prim and grey
I pound the bar and sing, 'Hooray,
Here's Quaker come to bless and kiss us,
Come, have a gin and bitters, missus.
Or maybe Quaker girls so prim
Would rather start a bloody hymn.
Now, Dick, oblige. A hymn, you swine
Pipe up the "officer of the line",
A song to make one's belly ache,
Or "Nell and Roger at the Wake",
Or that sweet song, the talk in town
"The lady fair and Abel Brown".
O, who's that knocking at the door.
Miss Bourne'll play the music score.
The men stood dumb as cattle are,
They grinned, but thought I'd gone too far,
There came a hush and no one break it,

99

They wondered how Miss Bourne would take it.
She up to me with black eyes wide,
She looked as though her spirit cried;
She took my tumbler from the bar
Beside where all the matches are
And poured it out upon the floor dust
Among the fag-ends, spit and sawdust.

'Saul Kane,' she said, 'when next you drink,
Do me the gentleness to think
That every drop of drink accursed
Makes Christ within you die of thirst,
That every dirty word you say
Is one more flint upon His way,
Another thorn about His head,
Another mock of where He tread,
Another nail, another cross,
All that you are is that Christ's loss.'
The clock run down and struck a chime
And Mrs Si said, 'Closing time'.

The wet was pelting on the pane
And something broke inside my brain,
I heard the rain drip from the gutters
And Silas putting up the shutters,
And one by one the drinkers went;
I got a glimpse of what it meant,
How she and I had stood before
In some old town by some old door
Waiting intent while someone knocked
Before the door for ever locked;
I heard her clang the Lion door,
I marked the drink-drop roll to floor;
It took up scraps of sawdust, furry,
And crinkled on, a half inch, blurry;
A drop from my last glass of gin;
And someone waiting to come in,
A hand upon the door latch gropin'
Knocking the man inside to open.[1]

★ ★ ★

Saul Kane opens the door to Christ. He is a changed man and all the Creation becomes
new to him through the everlasting mercy of Christ.

Thomas Kilner Braithwaite – G. Wilkie Gahan

G. Wilkie Gahan *was a Dundee poet and artist who wrote principally in Scots dialect. The following verses are taken from his book* The Trials of Truth and Other Words, *first published in 1915. The subject,* Thomas Kilner Braithwaite, *was at one time a master at Brookfield Friends School, Wigton. He retired to live at Barnhill in Dundee, where he was the only Quaker and the poem is of interest in revealing the impression he made on the community:*

O'ane, a Quaker, I maun speak,
His equal t'wad be hard tae seek,
An erudite and upricht man,
That's built upon the perfect plan;
Wi' reverence I lift the pen
Tae tackle this the 'King o' Men'.
A modest, yet a homely pride,
That suits him well what 'er betide,
His deference tae great an' sma'
Doth force respect from ane an' a;
He's cultured, scholarly, an' wise,
He loves the truth an' hates the lies.
He's ready aye tae hae a crack
As lang's ye keep upon the track
That carries frae the bad to better
An' leads towards the Scripture letter;
Fu' well the Bible he has read
Has made it quite his daily bread,
And by the laws therein laid doon,
He judges a' he sees aroon';
He kindly scans his brithers' failings,
Nor storms wi' curse their moral ailings.
A wise an' upricht judge he'd mak',
He'd scrutinise baith front and back,
He'd want to see a' roond aboot,
And then he'd turn it inside oot;
He'd want tae see the place it stands on,
And whaur the felon laid his hands on
In short – nae particle he'd miss,
Unless, of course, the Bible kiss;
In spite o' man or even wraith,
He ne'er wad brak' his honoured faith.
This micht dae weel if a' were Quakers,
But Lo'd keep me, there's lots o' fakirs
Wha only tell the truth because
They fear the Lord's revengeful laws;
But for this somewhat subtle point,

101

That maybe pits him oot o' joint,
I wadna frae my notion budge –
He'd mak' a grand an' upricht judge.
He kens the travels o' Saint Paul,
The Floods – The Plagues – and Adam's fall,
The Prophet's trials and Pharaoh's dream,
And Joseph's coat, ay, every seam,
The Ark – the Rod – and David's lyre,
The Prophets in the Holy fire,
The Altars made o' alabaster,
But crooning a' – he kens the Master.

(From Barnhill Lays)

DANGEROUS AGES – Rose Macaulay (c.1881-1958)

DANGEROUS AGES, which was first published in 1921, is a novel of four generations in a family and while the women's lives are described in detail the men's lives are only described as they relate to the women. The exception is Barry Briscoe, who appears as a suitor for Nan, eventually marrying her niece Gerda. Barry is the 'son of a famous Quaker philanthropist, and had been brought up to see good works done and even garden cities built,'[2] *but in Rose Macaulay's description of his own social involvement there is a suggestion of irony, of Quakerism adrift from its spiritual moorings in a sea of 'creaturely activity':*

Not even the rains of July 1920, made Barry weary or depressed. His eyes were bright behind his glasses; his hands were usually full of papers, committee reports, agenda, and the other foods he fed on, unsatiated and unashamed. Barry was splendid. What ardour, what enthusiasm, burning like beacons in a wrecked world! So wrecked a world that all but the very best and the very worst had given it up as a bad job; . . . But Barry, from the very heart of the ruin, would cry, 'Here is what we must do,' and his eyes would gleam with faith and resolution and he would form a committee to do it. And when he saw how the committee failed, as committees will, he would laugh ruefully and try something else. Barry, as he would tell you frankly if you enquired and not otherwise, believed in God.[3]

Quakerism as a religion with any depth of spirituality means nothing to him, there is no evidence that he attends a meeting for worship, the Quaker peace testimony did not prevent him from serving in the army in the first world war and he is an accomplished liar. He discards spiritual roots for socio/political fruits. Nevertheless, he has an unexpected effect on people——on Gerda, who worships him and joins him in his work, on Nan, cynical, 'fast':

Barry filled Nan, beneath her cynicism, beneath her levity, with something quite new——a queer desire, to put it simply, for goodness, for straight living and generous thinking, even, within reason, for usefulness. More and more he flooded her inmost being, drowning the old land-marks, like the sea at high tide. Nan was not a Christian, did not believe in God, but she came near at this time to believing in Christianity as a life, that it might be a fine and adventurous thing to live.[(4)]

In the whirlpool of the 1920's Rose Macaulay gives a picture of a Quaker, albeit lapsed, who somehow retains a shadow of Quaker plainness and integrity, so that he becomes an influence for good on those whose lives he touches. It is as if Quakerism itself had the possibility of working like a leaven within society at a time when spiritual values were in danger of being submerged in the feverish search for pleasure and material satisfaction.

THE EXILE 2, AUTUMN 1927 – *Ezra Pound (1885-1972)*

Taken from SELECTED PROSE *1909-1965, edited and with an* Introduction *by William Cookson.*[(5)]:

The drear horror of American life can be traced to two damnable roots, or perhaps it is only one root: 1. The loss of all distinction between public and private affairs. 2. The tendency to mess into other people's affairs before establishing order in one's own affairs, and in one's thoughts. To which one might perhaps add the lack in America of any habit of connecting or correlating any act or thought to any main principle whatsoever; the ineffable rudderlessness of that people. The principle of good is enunciated by Confucius; it consists in establishing order within oneself. This order or harmony spreads by a sort of contagion without specific effort. The principle of evil consists in messing with other people's affairs. Against this principle of evil no adequate precaution is taken by Christianity, Moslemism, Judaism, nor, as far as I know, by any monotheistic religion. Many 'mystics' do not even aim at the principle of good; they seek merely establishment of a parasitic relationship with the unknown. The original Quakers may have had some adumbration of the good principle.

THE QUAKER'S CELLO – Clifford Bax (1886-1962)

This one-act play, first published in 1933, is set in the back-parlour of a watch-maker's shop in a small market town in the year 1838. It has as its subject the Quaker condemnation of music, which was not allowed to be heard in the houses of many Quakers until late into the 19th century. The characters are Josiah Smallpiece, Rebecca *his wife and* Mary Medden, *a neighbour. Josiah, who before he became a Quaker was a member of the town band, possesses a violincello. He still has what he describes as an* 'unholy hunger for music', *which the two women regard as a lure of the senses. The play is concerned with Josiah's struggle against the temptation to play his 'cello and the efforts of the two women to overcome what they regard as a sin. Josiah finally concludes that the Lord requires him to burn his 'cello and he takes it out of the house to do this, but his heart fails him, he cannot destroy it and buries it deeply in the garden.*

The play highlights the difficulties which many Quakers with a leaning towards the arts must have experienced almost until the present century. Josiah can bury his 'cello until the Day of Judgment, but he cannot silence the longing for it in his soul.

IN GOOD KING CHARLES'S GOLDEN DAYS – Bernard Shaw (1856-1950)[6]

In this play, which was first published in 1939, Shaw wishes to portray Charles II as someone greater than the 'Merry Monarch' and collector of mistresses which he is often popularly held to be. So the play consists chiefly of imaginary conversations on science, religion and art between such figures as Newton, George Fox, Kneller *and* Charles *himself, the founder of the Royal Society. The play is set in the library of Isaac Newton at Cambridge in the year 1680. George Fox has come to visit Newton because he is concerned that science is contradicting scripture:*

Fox: Isaac Newton: I have friends who belong to the new so-called Royal Society which the king has established, to enquire, it seems, into the nature of the universe. They tell me things that my mind cannot reconcile with the word of God as revealed to us in the Holy Scriptures.

Newton: What is your warrant for supposing that revelation ceased when King James's printers finished with the Bible?

Fox: I do not suppose so. I am not one of those priestridden churchmen who believe that God went out of business six thousand years ago when he had called the world into existence and written his book about it. We three sitting here together may have a revelation if we open our hearts and minds to it. Yes: even to you, Charles Stuart.

Fox is shown as universalist in his belief and tolerant of Nell Gwynne, *whom he befriends:*

Fox: Sir: there is nobody who is not good enough for me. Have I not
          warned our Christian friends who are now captives in Barbary, not
          to forget that the life of God and the power of God are in their
          heathen masters the Turks and the Moors as well as in themselves?
          Is it any the less in this player woman than in a Turk or a Moor? I
          am not afraid of her,

and an exchange between Fox and Nell Gwynne (who is present) runs as follows:

Nell: Pray for me, Friend Fox: I think you have God by the ear closer than
          the bishop.

Fox: He is closer to you than you have placed yourself to me. Let no priest
          come between you.

Shaw gives Fox a speech in which he inveighs against the priesthood and is shown as loyal to Charles – 'He may be fifty times as clever as I; but so are many of the blackest villains. Value him rather for his flashes of the inner light. Did he not stop the butchering of the regicides on the ground that if he punished them they could never punish themselves?' *Fox is composed in the company of the king and Isaac Newton, although he regrets his lack of education. He is ready, if necessary, to be imprisoned again for conscience' sake. Shaw gives him a wide humanity, dignity and integrity, but to suggest that he found these qualities in 20th-century Friends would be speculation.*

SWAN SONG – *John Galsworthy (1867-1933)*

SWAN SONG *forms part of* THE FORSYTE CHRONICLE. *In this conversation between* Hilary Charwell *and his nephew* Michael Mont *Galsworthy makes the point that Quakers are likely to be concerned for the welfare of the poor and to support measures to alleviate the conditions under which they live:*

There's lots of room, of course, for slum area treatment by Borough Councils, and they do lots of good work, but by themselves, they'll never scotch the evil. You want the human touch; you want a sense of humour, and faith; and that's a matter for private effort in every town where there are slums . . . Surely, Michael, there must be ten just men who could be got to move in a matter like this . . . you could pinch a brace of bankers with Quaker blood in them . . .

---

edited by Alan Bishop and Aleksandra Bennet, 1989[7]

During the second world war Vera Brittain (1893-1970) *had close contacts with the Society of Friends. She was interested in the Society's relief work and wrote a report for Friends on* 'The Bedford Institutes in London's Blitzkrieg'. *She was also in contact during the war with* Roger Wilson *and with the* Friends Ambulance Unit. *The following brief extracts from her* Diary *show the esteem in which she held the Society*

Monday March 16th 1942: Very busy day with a good many letters. One long one from Corder Catchpool to which I replied at length, on the possibility twice discussed with him of my joining the Society of Friends. He invited me to go to their house at Highgate for a weekend and talk it over. Certainly to be supported by the strength of the Friends' organisation would be a wonderful experience, and a great one for me if I were worth their having.

Saturday April 18th 1942: . . . Went off after tea to spend the night with the Catchpools at Hampstead & discuss Quakerism. Their whole family – 3 girls and a small boy – were home from school, so after a long meal in the kitchen, music, etc., we didn't get to discussing the main topic till nearly midnight. By then I was almost too tired to be coherent, but did manage to express the doubt whether the Society, which is collectivist, was a suitable religious affiliation for the artist (whether writer, musician or painter), who is by nature individualistic, egotistical & exhibitionist. No conclusion reached by late bedtime.

THE PERENNIAL PHILOSOPHY – Aldous Huxley (1894-1963)

Aldous Huxley, *the author of such satirical novels as* CHROME YELLOW *and* THOSE BARREN LEAVES, *became one of the most serious and thoughtful of 20th-century writers.* THE PERENNIAL PHILOSOPHY, *first published in 1946, is an exploration of the constant presence of inner illumination, the theme of identity with the 'divine Reality', in the great religious traditions of the world. The following extracts from pages 223 and 224 present the Quaker concept of the Inner Light and, in the first of these, Huxley's view of its relation to Quaker pacifism:*

For the Quakers, soldiering was and is a form of wrong livelihood – war being, in their eyes, anti-Christian, not so much because it causes suffering as because it propogates hatred, puts a premium on fraud and cruelty, infects whole societies with anger, fear, pride and uncharitableness. Such passions eclipse the Inner Light, and therefore wars by which they are aroused and intensified must be regarded, whatever their immediate political outcome, as crusades to make the world safe for spiritual darkness.[8]

Of all Christian sects in the 17th century, the Quakers were the least obsessed by history, the least addicted to the idolatry of things in time. They believed that the inner light was in all human beings and that salvation came to those who lived in conformity with that light and was not dependent on the profession of belief in historical or pseudo-historical events, nor on the performance of certain rites, nor on the support of a particular ecclesiastical organization. Moreover, their eternity-philosophy preserved them from the materialistic apocalypticism of that progress-worship which in recent times has justified every kind of iniquity from war and revolution to sweated labour, slavery and the exploitation of savages and children——has justified them on the ground that the supreme good is in the future and that any temporal means, however intrinsically horrible, may be used to achieve that good. Because Quaker theology was a form of eternity-philosophy, Quaker political theory rejected war and persecution as means to ideal ends, denounced slavery and proclaimed racial equality. Members of other denominations had done good work for the African victims of the white man's rapacity. One thinks, for example, of St. Peter Claver of Cartagena. But this heroically charitable 'slave of the slaves' never raised his voice against the institution of slavery or the criminal trade by which it was sustained; nor, so far as the extant documents reveal, did he ever, like John Woolman, attempt to persuade slave-owners to free their human chattels.[9]

THE WORLD IN THE EVENING – *Christopher Isherwood (1904-1986)*

The greater part of this novel, which was first published in 1954, is set at the time of America's entry into the second world war and consists of the retrospective account of the first marriage of Stephen Monk, a wealthy Anglo-Indian. When Stephen finds his second wife Jane making love with another man at a Hollywood party he runs away from the situation and takes refuge with the Quaker he knows as 'Aunt Sarah', who was his foster-mother. Also staying with Aunt Sarah is Gerda Mannheim, a German refugee. Stephen and Gerda go to a Quaker meeting together and their experience is described as follows:

The grave white walls of the Meeting House, the hard plain benches, the Elders seated on a low facing gallery, the bowed heads and the Sunday hats. Late-comers found places hastily at the back and settled themselves, like chickens getting ready to roost. We had found Sarah waiting for us at the door, and had come in with her. Nobody looked at us directly, but it seemed to me that everyone was aware of our arrival . . .

. . . the Silence, in its old way, was coming to life. Was steadily filling up the bare white room, like water rising in a tank. Every one of us contributed to it, simply by being present. Togetherness grew and tightly enclosed us, until it seemed that we must all be breathing in unison and keeping time with our heart-beats. It was massively alive, and, somehow, unimaginably ancient, like the togetherness of Man in the primeval caves.[10]

THE LIVING OF THESE DAYS – *Harry Emerson Fosdick (1878-1969)*

In this autobiography the author, a minister at the non-sectarian, inclusive Riverside Church in New York, writes in 1957 of his attitude to the second world war, in which he hoped America would not become involved. The Wider Quaker Fellowship, to which he refers, distributed Quaker-oriented literature three times a year in English and once a year in Spanish to people in over 80 countries. Most are not Friends, but share an interest in the Quaker approach to life:

In the meantime, I had made many of my companions at Riverside Church unhappy by my attitude. They stood by me, but they were worried; and, anticipating what war, if it came, would do to my ministry, I worried too. I expected that it would mean, of course, my withdrawal from broadcasting and beyond that I prepared myself inwardly for the possible necessity of resigning from the church. In that case, my plan was clearly in mind——to join the Quakers and spend the rest of my life in their fellowship. If any one term best describes my position on war, it is to be called a Quaker. From its start I have been a member of the Wider Quaker Fellowship, and in the positive, constructive, socially-minded type of pacifism of the Society of Friends I find myself most at home.[11]

PILGRIMAGE – *Dorothy Richardson (1873-1957)*

Dorothy Richardson *is now regarded as one of the earliest authors in English of the 'stream of consciousness' form of writing, pre-dating the better known work of Virginia Woolf and James Joyce. Throughout her life she was engaged on a series of 13 novels which have been collectively entitled* PILGRIMAGE. *The story of* PILGRIMAGE, *which is fully autobiographical, is set in the 19th century and is told in the person of the young woman Miriam, who lives with a Quaker family until she has a love affair with their French protégé and is politely shown the door. The following extract provides a deeply sensitive description of the reaction of an outsider to a Quaker meeting for worship, culminating in a profound sense of spiritual unity:*

. . . Closing her eyes to concentrate upon the labour of retreat into stillness of mind and body, she recognised the iniquity of unpunctuality in attending a Quaker meeting. The room was utterly still. Half-way through the drawing of a deep breath, she was obliged to hamper the automatic movements of her limbs that with one accord were set on rearranging themselves. Stealthily her body straightened to sit upright, her head moved to relax the supporting muscles of her neck and came to rest a little bent. Lifted by a powerful circular movement of her shoulders that before she could restrain it had caused a gentle crackling of starched blouse-sleeves, her arms released themselves, unclasping her hands and setting them, with fingers relaxed, one upon each knee, while her feet, approaching each other, drew in just short of lifting their heels.

Even a beginning of concentration held an irrestible power. The next breath drew itself so deeply that she could prevent its outgoing from becoming a long, audible sigh only by holding and releasing it very gradually. It left her poised between the inner and the outer worlds, still aware of her surroundings and their strangeness and of herself as an alien element brought in by sympathetic understanding of the Quaker enterprise and engaged at last upon a labour whose immediate fruits were making her regret that it had not been, consciously, from the beginning of her life, her chief concern. To remain always centred, operating one's life, operating even its wildest enthusiasms from where everything fell into proportion and clear focus. To remain always in possession of a power that was not one's own, and yet one's own inmost being immediately recognised its centre.

Already she was aware of a change in her feeling towards those about her, a beginning of something more than a melting away of resentment towards the characteristics of some of those she had observed as she came into the room, an animosity now reversing itself by a movement of apology towards the woman on the platform and the dapper little man of ideas. Feeling now something more than a rationally tolerant indifference, something akin to the beginning of affection, she was free to take leave of them.

Why should it be only Quakers who employed, in public as well as privately, this approach to reality? Again, as at the beginning of the meeting she had attended in London, and where she had been little more than an interested spectator, she considered the enormity of breaking into sound the moment a congregation is assembled and keeping on, with scarcely an instant's breathing-space, until the end. 'For where two or three are gathered together in my name, there am I——in the midst of them'; to be immediately assailed by a torrent of words, confessions and protests, part-singing and the recital of poetic prayers, by readings aloud and at last by an address, compiled and delivered by one who may, or may not ever, have suffered a moment's religious experience.

What prevents the spreading, throughout Christendom, of a practice born of belief in the presence of God, necessarily following on that belief?

Be still and know. Still in mind as well as body. Not meditating, for meditation implies thought. Tranquil, intense concentration that reveals first its own difficulty, the main obstacles, and one's own weakness, and leads presently to contemplation, recognition.

Bidding her mind be still, she felt herself once more at work, in company, upon an all-important enterprise. This time her breathing was steady and regular and the labour of journeying, down through the layers of her surface being, a familiar process. Down and down through a series of circles each wider than the last, each opening with the indrawing of breath whose outward flow pressed her downwards towards the next, nearer to the living centre. Again thought touched her, comparing this research to a kind of mining operation. For indeed it was not flight. There was resistance from within, at once concrete and buoyant, a help and a hindrance, alternately drawing her forward and threatening, if for a moment her will relaxed, to drive her back amongst the distractions of the small cross-section of the visible world by which she was surrounded. And here, indeed, she was, up in her mind, open-eyed, everything about her very sharp and clear, though the room had darkened to a twilight . . .[12]

FATHER FIGURES – Kingsley Martin (1897-1969)

Kingsley Martin, *an influential former editor of the* NEW STATESMAN, *served with the* Friends Ambulance Unit *in France in 1917-18. Earlier in this book, which was published in 1966, he describes Quakerism as a* 'cranky religion'*:*

Quakers have always done well in business, most of all in chocolate and biscuits; trustworthy themselves, they have found that honesty is the best policy. Intermarrying, they have built a private aristocracy of their own, exclusive like other aristocracies, and calculated to make the outsider feel rather inferior. They have largely bred the artistic side out of themselves and neglected the graces of individual sympathy and friendship, though never in my experience refusing support for good causes. I should expect as much practical good will from the small body of Quakers as from all the other philanthropists put together. If I wanted companionship I should probably look elsewhere, though I was to meet individual Quakers whose friendship was neither niggardly nor confined.[13]

The Game – A. S. Byatt (1936-   )

This story, which was first published in 1967, is one of sibling rivalry, of an obses-
sional love/hate relationship between two sisters, Cassandra *and* Julia Corbett. *Their*
rivalry issues in professional competition and in the jealousy aroused by their relationship
with Simon, *whom they have both loved to the point of obsession from their girlhood.*
'The Game' *of the title is built by the two sisters on a childhood imaginative world of*
Mallory's knights, echoing the Gondal world of Emily and Anne Brontë. But this 'game'
becomes an allegory for the struggle between them and the novel opens with an act of betrayal
by Julia, who publishes a story based upon the 'game', in which both sisters had been
involved.

The sisters were born into a long-established and well-to-do Quaker family in
Northumberland, described as 'one of the oldest Quaker families, solid, unpreten-
tious, civilised bourgeoisie'.[14] *Their upbringing was tolerant, reasonable and full of*
choices they had to make, but they found this left them floundering——'The Inner Light
can indicate the edge of limitless darkness.[15]. *Both sisters leave the Society of Friends,*
Julia for no other religious denomination; Cassandra, however, feels the need for a frame-
work of ritual and liturgy to uphold her belief in God and turns to High Anglicanism. At
her last appearance in the meeting house at the age of 20 she rises 'pale and shivering'
to deliver an emotional denunciation of Quaker doctrine and particularly Friends' commit-
ment to non-violence, the 'too simple, idealistic view of human nature',[16] *what Julia*
describes as 'the way Friends familiarized the terrible and made it a comfortable
possession'.[17] *Cassandra's outburst was considered by the meeting to be 'unhelpful':*

You never question that it is possible for us to become good . . . You believe that
if we try to be good we shall affect things, make other people good. You appropriate the story of the Roman senators who sat so still that the Goths and Vandels
dared not touch them as a pacifist triumph . . . But this was no triumph of
anything but empty dignity, the Goths beat out the brains of those senators on
the marble pavement. You always talk as though passive resistance could convert
violence to love. But it can't, and it doesn't, and we ought to admit it. There *will*
always be people who will slash open the other cheek when it is turned to them.
In this life love *will not* overcome, it *will not*, it will go to waste and it is no good
to preach anything else. We need God because we are desperate and wicked and
can find Him only through Himself. The Inner Light doesn't necessarily shine,
and it doesn't illumine much.[18]

Later in the book Cassandra returns to the question of the Inner Light (p 101) and
the problem of non-violence is further explored in the character of Thor, *a Norwegian*
Quaker whom Julia marries. Thor works for an international charity with which Quakers
are connected and carries his concern to live out his faith to the extent of bringing back a
homeless family to his own house. Eventually he is asked to go out to the Congo to do
relief work, but Julia refuses to go with him and his non-violent principles collapse. He
goes berserk and finally shouts at her – 'I want to break your neck, too, that's a fact,
and I'm going before I do'.[19] *He is described early in the novel as having the* 'capacity to swallow abruptly any momentary anger',[20] *but this smothering of anger is*

against his true nature; he has tried too hard to obey principles which intellectually he approves and is described by Simon as:

an immoderate man brought up in a tradition of moderation. So he was immoderate about that too. A naturally violent man, a fanatic, trying to be a reasonable pacifist.[21]

Both Cassandra's words and Thor's behaviour make the point that pacifism is sometimes impotent against the capacity for violence innate to a greater or lesser degree in the human psyche and that indeed the long drawn out attempt to contain it may result in an explosion of rage far greater than is warranted by a situation.

THE AUTOBIOGRAPHY OF BERTRAND RUSSELL (1872-1970)

Bertrand Russell's AUTOBIOGRAPHY, which was published in 1968, has references to his contact with Quakers, notably during the first world war. The following extract describes his encounter with Edward Grubb, the national treasurer of the No Conscription Fellowship founded by Fenner Brockway, who described him as the 'father of the movement':

There were some among the Quakers whom I admired very greatly, in spite of a very different outlook. I might take as typical of these the treasurer of the No Conscription Fellowship, Mr Grubb . . . He acted on behalf of young men in prison with a complete absence of even the faintest trace of self-seeking. When he and a number of others were being prosecuted for a pacifist publication, my brother was in court. My brother, though not a pacifist, was impressed by the man's character and integrity.[22]

EXPERIENCES – Arnold Toynbee (1889-1975)

In the extract quoted from this book Arnold Toynbee *looks back to the South African War and to the stand made for the Quaker peace testimony by* George Cadbury:

However, in Britain when I was a child mankind's traditional attitude towards war was still almost universally prevalent there. At that time the only Westerners who regarded war as being a criminal institution, and who refused resolutely to have any part or lot in it, were the members of the Society of Friends. This stand that was taken by the Quakers was respected by people who differed from them

112

in taking what was then the normal view. It was recognized that the Quakers were utterly sincere in holding the moral convictions they held; that they had some other peculiar moral convictions besides their queer notion that war is a crime; and that they were prepared to suffer for remaining true to their convictions when the test came.

The Quakers did stand up to the test. An example is the stand taken by the Quaker chocolate-manufacturer, Mr. George Cadbury, during the South African War – a British war that was as controversial and invidious as the American war in Vietnam. In taking this courageous stand on principle, Mr. Cadbury was not only voluntarily denying to himself particular contracts that would have been financially profitable; he was also incurring public odium in Britain to a degree at which this threatened to damage his business as a whole; for, in a war that the British were waging with a bad conscience, their usual respect for people who resist temptations to act against their conscience was temporarily overborne by chauvinism. The moral conflict between Mr. Cadbury and the pro-war majority of the British public was a conflict between the post-Christian Western religion of Nationalism and a small community of Christians who were peculiar in obeying the commandments that are attributed to Jesus in the Christian Gospels.

The Quakers did, and do, set a moral example to their fellow human beings. Yet the Quakers were, and are, only a handful among the English-speaking minority of the Protestant minority of the officially Christian minority of mankind. The Quakers are a yeast which has not yet leavened the lump – though human history presents some striking illustrations of the eventual triumph, contrary to all apparent likelihood, of principles held by tiny minorities who have stood for these principles whole-heartedly and who have therefore been prepared to suffer for their principles to any extent. Time and again, martyrdom has proved more potent than the physical force that is wielded by governments.[23]

A PLACE APART –Dervla Murphy (1931-

In the spring of 1976 the Irish writer Dervla Murphy *decided to visit Northern Ireland. While she was there she was invited to stay with a family whom she subsequently found to be Quakers and the following extract illustrates the unique position the Society holds in the Province in its capacity to engage in dialogue with each party, entirely free from partisanship:*

Towards the end of my time in Northern Ireland I had a strange little experience. I had been invited to stay with a family of whom I knew nothing, in a town I had not visited before, and the surname was to my ears 'theologically' neutral. When I telephoned to announce my time of arrival an elderly man spoke

113

to me and during our brief conversation I got the impression of unusual gentleness and warmth. At dusk I found the neat little bungalow and immediately realised that this was not a Catholic home——but neither was it Northern Irish Protestant. I felt sure of that because of the family's demeanour ('aura' would be a better word but it makes people laugh). Yet everybody had a marked Northern accent and the whole thing was quite baffling.

As we talked I found myself communicating without any constraint, as I would have done among old friends. 'Atmosphere' is something that has fascinated me in many parts of the world; it is so definite and yet so indefinable. In that atmosphere I was aware of relaxing completely, as I had not done for what seemed like a long time. The familiar Northern tension was not there and I felt no need to be careful lest I give offence. Then, after a few hours, the mystery was solved by a chance remark. I was among Quakers.[24]

THE PHILOSOPHER'S PUPIL – *Iris Murdoch (1919-   )*

This novel, first published in 1983, is based round the McCaffrey family, whose Quakerism has worn thin or is non-existent. In the opening sequence the anti-hero George McCaffrey, the pupil of the title, is shown as consumed with hatred for the wife whom he tried to drown and with few exceptions the main characters are portrayed as vain, selfish, proud or sentimental. All are fallen away from religious faith, are lapsed Quakers, lapsed Methodists, lapsed Anglicans. An exception is the Quaker William Eastcote, a pillar of his meeting, who is depicted as a good and saintly man. Ministry he gives at a Friends' meeting deeply impresses those present and the following brief extract may give some idea of Iris Murdoch's presentation of the Quaker approach to the religious life:

. . . Repentance, renewal of life, such as is the task and possibility of every man, is a recovery of innocence. Let us see it thus, a return to a certain simplicity, something which is not hard to understand, not a remote good, but very near. . . Let us prize chastity, not as a censorious or rigid code, but as fastidious respect and gentleness . . . a sense of the delicate mystery of human relations . . . Conversion is turning about, and it can happen not only every day but every moment. Shun the cynicism which says that our world is so terrible that we may as well cease to care and cease to strive, the notion of a cosmic crisis where ordinary duties cease to be and moral fastitiousness is out of place. At any time, there are many many small things we can do for other people which will refresh us and them with new hope . . . Recognize one's own evil, mend what can be mended, and for what cannot be undone, place it in love and faith in the clear light of the healing goodness of God.[25]

The book contains a sensitive account of a Friends' meeting for worship. One of the characters, who loves the silence, describes it as:

healing waves lapped in a slow rhythm against the scratched and smarting soul. [26]

But apparently dogs could also be regarded as recipients of the Inner Light. Zed, a little pet dog, is taken to a meeting for worship:

Why should not dogs be present, since the waves and particles of the Inner Light flowed through them too? [27]

George's half-brother Tom, a much younger, cheerful, out-going young man, a Quaker by upbringing but drawn away by the 'world's vanities', is horrified to discover that he has inner demons and is capable of hatred, while the presentation of George's brother Brian hints at some of the tensions which trouble the Society today. Brian is a member of a Quaker meeting; he does not believe in God, but:

. . . Ennistone Friends were not anxious about the matter. The Mystery of God was one with the Inner Light of the Soul, and the illumined Way was the Good Life, where truthful vision spontaneously prompted virtuous desire. [28]

George McCaffrey pursues his long progress through the book, from the hatred and anger which consume him at the beginning to his final conversion experience. But his change of heart is due to a sudden shock, an almost Pauline experience inexplicable in its origin. There is no slow return to his lapsed Quaker faith, only the realisation that he needs, as William Eastcote knew so well, the forgiveness of God, repentance and renewal of life.

---

98 NOT OUT – Fenner Brockway (1888-1988)

The Society's historic peace testimony has been and still is a dominant theme in Quaker thought and work during the present century and it is fitting that this anthology should close with a tribute from Fenner Brockway in the following extract from his last book, published in 1986. In January 1982, in connection with the World Disarmament Campaign, Fenner Brockway was invited by the Northern Friends Peace Board to join a peace mission to the then Soviet Union. He describes the Quaker involvement as follows:

Before we went the Quakers asked permission to criticize Soviet policy as openly as we criticized British policy. To my surprise, this request was accepted by the Soviet Peace Committee and we expressed our views on Afghanistan, Poland, the dissidents and conscientious objectors, not only in committee but at meetings. The only censorship was by the Soviet media which reported what we said in commendation but not in criticism.

A success achieved by the Quaker Peace Mission also surprised me. I proposed to my colleagues that we should submit a programme to the Soviet Peace

Committee for joint signature. After discussion they agreed to a draft. It began by endorsing the recommendations of the first UN Special Session, thus accepting the objectives of the WDC (UK) and then listed a series of measures leading to the simultaneous abolition of NATO and the Warsaw Pact.

When we met the Soviet Committee, its members had no hesitation in accepting our draft with only minor amendments and insisted on adding a final clause, calling on all nations to endorse the United Nations declaration that a nuclear war would be a crime against humanity.[29]

REFERENCES AND NOTES

INTRODUCTION

[1] Susan Doran and Christopher Durston: *PRINCES, PASTORS AND PEOPLE, THE CHURCH AND RELIGION IN ENGLAND, 1529-1689*, 1991, p 116 (by permission of Routledge).
[2] W. C. Braithwaite: *THE BEGINNING OF QUAKERISM*, 1992, p 411.
[3] London Yearly Meeting Epistles, 1700-c.1720.
[4] P. C. Lipscomb; William Pitt and the Slave Trade, pp 79-80; LSF MIC 104.
[5] *See* Nancy Boyd: *THREE VICTORIAN WOMEN WHO CHANGED THEIR WORLD*, OUP 1982.

CHAPTER I

[1] E. H. W. Meyerstein (editor) 1945: *ADVENTURES BY SEA* by Edward Coxere, pp 86-87 (by permission of Oxford University Press).
[2] op cit p 90.
[3] Antonia Fraser: *THE WEAKER VESSEL*, 1984, p 264 (by permission of George Weidenfeld & Nicholson Ltd).
[4] op cit p 356.
[5] op cit p 357.
[6] John Punshon: *PORTRAIT IN GREY*, 1984, p 59 (by permission of the author).
[7] Antonia Fraser, op cit pp 357-358.

CHAPTER II

[1] The Questions raised by 'The Fair Quakers' and its sequel are considered in a study prepared by Derek Forbes, to whom I am indebted for this material, under the title *THE ENIGMA OF JOHN BINGLEY'S POEM 'THE FAIR QUAKERS' (1773)*. This study and the full text of the poem may be consulted at Friends House Library, London, or on application to Friends Meeting House, Railway Street, Hertford.
[2] The material in this account is taken from *THE STAGING OF QUAKERS IN EIGHTEENTH CENTURY DRAMA*, by Derek Forbes, a paper delivered to Friends at Hertford Meeting House on 1 July 1991. The full paper is available at Friends House Library, London, accession no. 10316 and at Woodbrooke College Library.

CHAPTER III

[1] *LETTERS OF CHARLES AND MARY LAMB*, edited by E. V. Lucas, vol 1, p 101.
[2] Ibid.

³ op cit p 376.
⁴ op cit p 193.
⁵ Hesketh Pearson: *THE SMITH OF SMITHS*, 1977, p 147 (by permission of Michael Holroyd)
⁶ Peter Medawar: *INDUCTION AND INTUITION IN SCIENTIFIC THOUGHT*, 1969 (by permission of The American Philosophical Society).

CHAPTER IV

¹ John Masefield: *THE EVERLASTING MERCY*, 1911 (by permission of The Society of Authors as the literary representative of the Estate of John Masefield).
² Rose Macaulay: *DANGEROUS AGES*, 1921, p 56 (by permission of Methuen, London).
³ op cit p 57.
⁴ op cit p 149.
⁵ William Cookson (editor): *SELECTED PROSE*, 1909-1965 (Copyright (c) 1960, 1962 by Ezra Pound) used by permission of New Directions Publishing Corporation and Faber & Faber Ltd.
⁶ Bernard Shaw: *IN GOOD KING CHARLES'S GOLDEN DAYS*, 1939 (by permission of The Society of Authors on behalf of the Bernard Shaw Estate).
⁷ The extracts from *WARTIME CHRONICLE: VERA BRITTAIN'S WAR DIARY, 1939-1945* are included by permission of Victor Gollancz Ltd, Alan Bishop and Y. Aleksandra Bennett, the editors, and Paul Berry, Vera Brittain's literary executor.
⁸ Aldous Huxley: *THE PERENNIAL PHILOSOPHY*, 1946, p. 137 (by permission of Mrs Laura Huxley, the source, Chatto & Windus and Harper Collins, Publishers).
⁹ op cit pp 223-224.
¹⁰ Christopher Isherwood: *THE WORLD IN THE EVENING*, 1954, pp 50-51 (reproduced with permission of Curtis Brown Group Ltd, copyright the Estate of Christopher Isherwood, 1954).
¹¹ Harry Emerson Fosdick: *THE LIVING OF THESE DAYS*, 1957, p 295 (by permission of the SCM Press).
¹² Dorothy Richardson: *PILGRIMAGE 4*, pp 497-499 (copyright under the Berne Convention; published by Virago Press Ltd in 1979. Also by permission of the University of Illinois Press).
¹³ Kingsley Martin: *FATHER FIGURES*, 1966, p 69 (by permission of Peters Fraser & Dunlop Group Ltd).
¹⁴ A. S. Byatt: *THE GAME*, 1967, p 34 (by permission of Chatto & Windus and reprinted by permission of Peters Fraser & Dunlop Group Ltd).
¹⁵ op cit p 41.
¹⁶ op cit p 38.
¹⁷ op cit p 37.
¹⁸ op cit p 38.
¹⁹ op cit p 186.
²⁰ op cit p 62.
²¹ op cit p 168.
²² Bertrand Russell: *AUTOBIOGRAPHY*, 1968, vol 2, pp 38-39 (by permission of Allen & Unwin)
²³ Arnold Toynbee: *EXPERIENCES*, 1969, pp 209-211 (by permission of Oxford University Press)

[24] Dervla Murphy: *A PLACE APART,* 1978, pp 103-104 (by permission of John Murray, Publisher. Also Copyright by Devin-Adair, Publishers, Inc., Old Greenwich, Connecticut, 06870. Permission granted to reprint from *A PLACE APART,* by Dervla Murphy. All rights reserved).

[25] Iris Murdoch: *THE PHILOSOPHER'S PUPIL,* 1983, pp 204-205 [by permission of Chatto & Windus; Also from *THE PHILOSOPHER'S PUPIL* by Iris Murdoch, Copyright (c) 1983, by Iris Murdoch (used by permission of Viking Penguin, a division of Penguin Books USA Inc.)].

[26] op cit p 198.

[27] op cit p 20.

[28] op cit p 54.

[29] Fenner Brockway: *98 NOT OUT,* 1986, pp 85-86 (by permission of Quartet Books Ltd).

CONTRIBUTORS TO THE ANTHOLOGY

Elizabeth Alley

Edrey Allott

Gwyn E. Arveschoeg

Walter Bagshot

Renault Beakbane

David Blamires

Emma Bodycote

Robert Barclay Braithwaite

Penelope Bray

Peter Brook

Peter Tatton Brown

Alex Bryan

Hester Burton

Kathleen Cottrell

Helen Davidson

Kathleen Edwards

Robin Evelyn

Clifford du Feu

Derek Forbes

Rachel Forti

Stephanie Gifford

Margaret Glover

Margaret Gough

David Hall

Arthur Hewlett

Alec Holmes

Margaret Hughes

Michael Hughes

Barbara Jennings

Joanna Kirkby

Ken Knight

John Lampen

Laurence Lerner

Vera Massey

William Matchett

Edward H. Milligan

Cherry Morton

John Nicholson

Arthur Olerenshaw

Ted Parrott

Rachel Pearse

Thomas Penny

Else Pickvance

Matilda Popper

Sue Proudlove

Stuart Randall

Barbara Noel Scott

Audrey J. Smith

Raymond South

Neil Stuart

Polly Tatum

Ben Vincent

Ronald Walker

Patricia Watkins

Janet Wells

Winifred White

Eric Wood

Martin Wyatt

Robert Yearly

INDEX

ADVENTURES by Sea (Coxere), 4ff
Allen, William, 72
Antiquities and Memoirs of Myddle (Gough), 13f
Anti-slavery Committee, The, x, 79
Apology, The (Barclay), viii, 31
Arouet, François Marie (Voltaire), 28
Autobiography of Bertrand Russell, The, 112

BARBER, Margaret Fairless: *see* Fairless, Michael
Barclay, Robert, viii, 21, 31
Barton, Bernard, 58, 59, 74
Bax, Clifford, 104
Baxter, Richard, vii, 9, 11: *Autobiographical writings,* 11f
Bellers, John, ix
Benezet, Anthony, 46
Bentham, Jeremy, 48
Bewick, Thomas: *Memoir of,* 71
Bingley, John, 17
Blackwood's Magazine, 74
Blamires, David, viii, 7, 20
Bold Stroke for a Wife, A (Centlivre), 48ff
Borrow, George, x, 82f
Boswell, James, 40ff
Brittain, Vera, xi, 106
Brockway, Fenner, xi, 115
Brontë, Charlotte, 80
Bunyan, John, 2
Burrough, Edward, viii, 5
Butler, Josephine, x
Buxton, Sir Thomas Fowell, x: *Memoir of,* 78ff

Byat, A. S., xi, 111
Byron, Lord, ix, 60

CADBURY, George, xi, 113
Captain Singleton (Defoe), 27f
Carlyle, Thomas, x, 72f
Catchpool, Corder, xi, 106
Centlivre, Susannah, 48f
Chetwood, William Rufus, 50
Clarendon Code, The, viii
Clarkson, Thomas, 46
Cobbett, William, x, 65
Coleridge, Samuel Taylor, 76
Conway, Anne, viii, 8
Coxere, Edward, 4f
Craik, Mrs: *see* Mulock, Dinah Maria

DANGEROUS Ages (Macaulay), xi, 102f
Defoe, Daniel, viii, 24, 26ff, 46
Diary of Samuel Pepys, The, 3
Dibden, Charles, 52
Directory of Public Worship, The, viii, 8
Drama, 18th-century, 48ff
Dyer, Mary, 9

ELLWOOD, Thomas, 1
Essay on Slavery and Commerce of the Human Species (Clarkson), 46f
Ettrick Shepherd, The, 74
Evelyn, John, vii, 1
Everlasting Mercy, The (Masefield), 99f
Exile, The (Pound), 103
Experiences (Toynbee), 112f

FAIR Quaker of Deal, The
  (Shadwell), 45, 48f
Fair Quakers, The (Bingley), ix, 17ff
Fairless, Michael, x, 95
Father Figures (Martin), 110
Fell, Margaret, 8
Fielding, Henry, 32
Fiennes, Celia, viii, 6
Fisher, Mary, 8, 9
Fisher, Samuel, 5
Forbes, Derek, viii, 48
Fosdick, Harry Emerson, xi, 108
Fox, George, vii, viii, ix, 1, 84, 98,
  104f
Fraser, Antonia, 8, 9
Fry, Elizabeth, x, 53, 78

GAHAN, G. Wilkie, 101
Galsworthy, John, 105
Galton, Francis, 94
Game, The (Byatt), xi, 111f
Gaskell, Mrs, viii, ix, 93
Gentleman's Magazine, The, 36ff
Gough, Richard, 13
*Grace Abounding for the Chief of
  Sinners* (Bunyan), 2
Green, Matthew, viii, 21
Greville, Charles Cavendish Fulke:
  Memoirs, 72
Grey Brethren, The (Fairless), 95f
Grubb, Edward, xi, 112
Gurney, John, 78f
Gurney, Joseph John *(footnote 78),* 84

HAZLITT, William, 63
Hill, Octavia, x
Hogg, James, 74
Hooton, Elizabeth, 8, 9
Howard, Luke (1621-1699), 5
Howgill, Francis, viii
Hume, David, ix, 34
Huxley, Aldous, 106

IMPERFECT Sympathies (Lamb), 58
In Good King Charles's Golden Days
  (Shaw), 104f

*Induction and Intuition in Scientific
  Thought* (Medwar), 94
*Introduction to Principles of Morals and
  Legislation* (Bentham), 18
Isherwood, Christopher, xi, 107

JAMES, William, 98
Japhet in Search of a Father (Marryat),
  45, 77
John Endicott (Longfellow), 84ff
John Halifax, Gentleman (Mulock:
  Mrs Craik), x, 90
John Tregenoweth His Mark (Pearse),
  81f
Johnson, Life of (Boswell), 40ff
Journal of the Plague Year (Defoe), 24
Journals of Dorothy Wordsworth, The
  60
Journeys of Celia Fiennes, The, 6ff

*KINGDOM of God is Within You,
  The* (Tolstoy), 96f

LAMB, Charles, 58, 59, 61
Lavengro (Borrow), 82f
Letters from England (Southey), 61ff
Lettres philosophique (Voltaire), 28ff
*Life and Times of Anthony à Wood,
  The,* 1f
Living of These Days, The (Fosdick),
  108
Lloyd, Charles, 58
London Yearly Meeting, x
Longfellow, Henry Wadsworth, 84
Lover, Samuel, 91
Lover's Opera, The (Chetwood), 48

MACAULAY, Rose, x, xi, 102
Marryat, Captain, 77
Martin, Kingsley, 110
Masefield, John, 99
Maud (Tennyson), 89
Medawar, Peter, 94
Meeting for Sufferings, 39f
Melville, Herman, 86

Moby Dick (Melville), 86ff
Moll Flanders (Defoe), 24f, 46
Mulock, Dinah Maria (Mrs Craike),
  x, 90
Murdoch, Iris, xi, 114f
Murphy, Dervla, 113

NATURAL History of Selborne, The
  (White), 36
Naylor, James, 49
New England Tragedies (Longfellow),
  84
98 Not Out (Brockway), 115f
No Conscription Fellowship, xi,
  112
No Cross, No Crown (Penn), 58
Noctes Ambrosiana (Wilson &
  others), 74ff
North, Christopher, 74
Northcote's Conversations (Hazlitt),
  63ff
Northern Friends Peace Board, xi,
  115

O'KEEFFE, John, 52
Of Superstition and Enthusiasm
  (Hume), 34f
On Barclay's Apology for the Quakers
  (Green), 21ff
One Sheet Against the Quakers
  (Baxter), 9ff
Orders in Council, The, 80

PAST and Present (Carlyle), 72f
Pearse, Mark Guy, 81, 82
Penn, William, 4, 12, 31, 58, 84
Pepys, Samuel, 3, 9
Perennial Philosophy, The (Huxley),
  106f
Philosopher's Pupil, The (Murdoch),
  114f
Pilgrimage (Richardson), 108ff
Pilgrim's Progress, The (Bunyan), 3
Place Apart, A (Murphy), 113f
Pound, Ezra, 103
Punshon, John, 8

QUAKER Meeting, A (Lamb), 58
Quaker Miscellany for Edward
  Milligan, A, 7, 20
Quaker, The (Dibden), 52
Quaker, The (a 'Lady'), 44ff
Quaker's Cello, The (Bax), 104
Quaker's Meeting, The (Lover), x, 91f
Quakers Observed in Prose and Verse
  (Blamires), 7, 20

REDGAUNTLET (Scott), 67ff, 77
Richardson, Dorothy, 108
Round Table, The (Hazlitt), 63ff
Roxana (Defoe), 25ff
Rural Rides (Cobbett), 65ff
Russell, Bertrand, viii, xi, 112

SANDY Foundation Shaken, A
  (Penn), 4
Scott, Sir Walter, 67
Shadwell, Charles, 48
Shaw, Bernard, 104
Shirley (Brontë), 80ff
Smith of Smiths, The (Ed. Michael
  Holroyd), 78
Smith, Sydney, x, 78
Southey, Robert, 61
Spectator, The, no. 132, 14ff
Statistical Inquiry into the Efficacy of
  Prayer (Galton), 94
Steele, Richard, 17, 18
Sterling, John, Life of (Carlyle), 73
Swan Song (Galsworthy), 105
Sylvia's Lovers (Gaskell), viii, ix, 93f

TABLE Talk and Omniana
  (Coleridge), 76
Tennyson, Alfred Lord, 89
Thomas Kilner Braithwaite (Gahan),
  101f
To a Beautiful Quaker (Byron), ix,
  60f
To a Virgin Speaker Among the
  Quakers (Philanthropos), 37ff
To the Spade of a Friend
  (Wordsworth), 43f

Toleration Act, ix
Tolstoy, Leo, 96
Tom Jones (Fielding), 32ff
Toynbee, Arnold, x, xi, 112
Truth Exalted (Penn), 4

*VARIETIES of Religious Experience,
The* (James), 98
Voltaire, 28ff, 61

WARTIME Chronicle, 1939-1945
(Brittain), 106
Weaker, Vessel, The (Fraser), 8f
Westminster Review, The: July 1869,
94

White, Gilbert, 36
Whitney, Janet, 53
Wilberforce, William, x, 79
Wild Oats (O'Keefe), 52
Wild Wales (Borrow), 83f
Wilkinson, Thomas, 43
Wilson, John, 74
Wood, Anthony à, vii, 1, 5
Woolman, John, 46, 58
Wordsworth, Dorothy, 60
Wordsworth, William, 43, 76
World in the Evening, The
(Isherwood), 107f